Quest

Teacher's Edition

2

 **Reading and Writing**

Student Book Author
Pamela Hartmann

Teacher's Edition Writer
Kristin Sherman

 **McGraw-Hill**

Quest 2 Reading and Writing Teacher's Edition

Published by McGraw-Hill ESL/ELT, a business unit of The McGraw-Hill Companies, Inc., 1221 Avenue of the Americas, New York, NY 10020.

ISBN 978-0-07-326580-3
MHID 0-07-326580-2
3 4 5 6 7 8 9 QPD/QPD 12 11 10 09 08 07

Editorial director: Erik Gundersen
Series editor: Linda O'Roke
Development editor: Jennifer Bixby
Production manager: Juanita Thompson
Production coordinator: MaryRose Malley
Cover designer: David Averbach, Anthology
Interior designer: Karolyn Wehner

www.esl-elt.mcgraw-hill.com

TABLE OF CONTENTS

●●●●●● WELCOME to the Teacher's Edition

The *Quest* Teacher's Edition provides support and flexibility to teachers using the *Quest* Student Book. Each chapter of the Teacher's Edition begins with a chapter overview that includes a brief summary of the Student Book chapter, a list of the vocabulary words found in the chapter, a list of the reading, critical thinking, and writing strategies highlighted throughout the chapter, as well as a list of the mechanics presented and practiced in that chapter. In addition, the Teacher's Edition provides step-by-step teaching procedures; answer keys; notes on culture, grammar, vocabulary, and pronunciation; tips for the TOEFL® iBT; expansion activities; photocopiable masters of select expansion activities; website research ideas; and end-of-chapter tests.

Procedures

○ Experienced teachers can use the step-by-step procedural notes as quick guides and refreshers before class, while newer or substitute teachers can use the notes as a more extensive guide in the classroom. These notes also help teachers provide context for the activities and assess comprehension of the material covered.

Answer Keys

○ Answer keys are provided for all activities that have definite answers. In cases where multiple answers could be correct, possible answers are included. Answer keys are also provided for the Vocabulary Workshop after each unit.

Notes

○ Where appropriate, academic culture, grammar, vocabulary, and pronunciation notes provide background information, answers to questions students might raise, or points teachers might want to review or introduce. For example, in *Quest Level 2 Reading and Writing* Chapter 1, a reading refers to Nike, so a cultural note provides some background information on this company. These notes are provided at the logical point of use, but teachers can decide if and when to use the information in class.

TOEFL® iBT Tips

○ In each chapter, six tips for the TOEFL iBT are given with corresponding notes on how strategies and activities from the student book chapter can help students practice and prepare for the exam. Examples of TOEFL iBT question format are also given in these tips.

Expansion Activities

○ At least 10 optional expansion activities are included in each chapter. These activities offer teachers creative ideas for reinforcing the chapter content while appealing to different learning styles. Activities include games, conversation practice, and working with manipulatives such as sentence strips, projects, and presentations. These expansion activities often allow students to practice all four language skills, not just the two skills that the student book focuses on.

TOEFL is a registered trademark of Educational Testing Service (ETS). This publication is not endorsed or approved by ETS.

Photocopiable Masters

○ Up to three black line masters that teachers can photocopy are included for each chapter. These worksheets are optional and are described in expansion activities located within the chapter. One chapter worksheet is often additional editing practice, while the others might be a graphic organizer or a set of sentence strips.

Website Research

○ At the end of Part 3 in each chapter of the Teacher's Edition, you will find a list of suggested website resources that can provide additional information on the topics presented in the chapter. Teachers may use this optional resource to gather more background or to direct students to these sites to research the topics for an expansion activity. The title of each suggested website is given and can be searched if the listed website is unavailable.

End-of-Chapter Tests

○ The end-of-chapter tests assess students on reading comprehension, one or more of the reading or critical thinking strategies highlighted in the chapter, vocabulary, mechanics, and editing. Item types include multiple choice, fill-in-the-blank, and true/false, for a total of 35 items per test. Answer keys are provided.

Scope and Sequence

Chapter	Reading Strategies	Writing Strategies
UNIT 1 BUSINESS		
Chapter 1 **Doing Business Internationally** • Introduction: *International Marketing Mistakes* • General Interest Reading: *International Culture* • Academic Reading: *Improving CQ: Understanding Cultural Values*	• Understanding New Words • Dealing with New Words • Guessing the Meaning from Context: Punctuation • Predicting • Finding the Main Idea • Finding Details • Thinking Ahead • Guessing the Meaning from Context: Using Logic • Using Graphic Organizers: Venn Diagrams and Charts	• Focus: Writing an Expository Paragraph • Strategy: Making Inferences
Chapter 2 **The Global Economy** • Introduction: *The Exchange of Material Goods* • General Interest Reading: *Excerpt from Lawrence Durrell's* Bitter Lemons • Academic Reading: *Economic Systems*	• Previewing for Topics • Guessing the Meaning from Context: Accepting Incomplete Knowledge • Understanding Parts of Speech • Guessing the Meaning from Context • Keeping a Word Journal • Guessing the Meaning from Context: Using the Next Sentence • Marking a Textbook • Finding the Topic Sentence • Using Graphic Organizers: Charts	• Focus: Writing a Paragraph of Analysis • Strategy: Writing a Topic Sentence

The Mechanics of Writing	Critical Thinking Strategies	Test-Taking Strategies
UNIT 1 BUSINESS		
• Simple Present and Simple Past • Modals of Advice • The Subject *You* • Adjective Clauses • Transitional Expressions: Coordinating Conjunctions	• Thinking Ahead • Making Inferences	• Finding Details • Guessing the Meaning from Context: Using Logic • Finding Errors • Editing a Test Essay
• The Passive Voice • Transitional Expressions: Adverbial Conjunctions • Recognizing and Repairing Run-Ons and Comma Splices	• Synthesizing and Applying Information • Using Graphic Organizers: Charts	• Understanding Parts of Speech • Guessing the Meaning from Context

Scope and Sequence

Chapter	Reading Strategies	Writing Strategies
UNIT 2 ART		
Chapter 3 **Themes and Purposes** • Introduction: *Looking at Art: What's the Story?* • General Interest Reading: *The Sacred Realm of Art* • Academic Reading: *Art as the Mirror of Everyday Life*	• Determining Point of View • Guessing the Meaning from Context: Pictures and Captions • Finding Main Ideas: Major Sub-Topics • Understanding Italics	• Focus: Writing a Paragraph of Comparison-Contrast • Strategy: Gathering Supporting Material
Chapter 4 **The Ancient World: Egypt** • Introduction: *The Rules of Egyptian Art* • General Interest Reading: *Finds Reveal Much of Life at Pyramids* • Academic Reading: *Egyptian Civilization: A Brief History*	• Guessing the Meaning from Context: Using Opposites • Recognizing Style: Newspaper Feature Stories • Guessing the Meaning from Context: *in other words, that is, i.e.* • Finding Evidence	• Focus: Writing a Paragraph of Cause and Effect
UNIT 3 PSYCHOLOGY		
Chapter 5 **States of Consciousness** • Introduction: *Lucid Dreaming* • General Interest Reading: *Dreaming Across Cultures* • Academic Reading: *The Function and Meaning of Dreaming*	• Understanding Ellipses • Having Questions in Mind • Finding the Topic Sentence • Choosing the Correct Dictionary Definition	• Focus: Writing a Paragraph of Analysis • Strategy: Writing About Symbols • Strategy: Gathering and Organizing Ideas • Strategy: Using Graphic Organizers: Idea Maps

The Mechanics of Writing	Critical Thinking Strategies	Test-Taking Strategies
UNIT 2 ART		
• Appositives • Adjective Clauses • Participial Phrases • Prepositional Phrases • Adjectives • Order of Adjectives • Transitional Expressions: Comparison-Contrast	• Comparing and Contrasting Two Works of Art • Determining Point of View	• Understanding Pronouns
• Infinitives of Purpose • Transitional Expressions of Cause and Effect: Subordinating Conjunctions • Transitional Expressions and Phrases • Conjunctions of Cause and Effect: Review	• Identifying Causes and Effects • Finding Evidence	• Understanding Idioms • Applying Information
UNIT 3 PSYCHOLOGY		
• Transitional Words of Time • Verbs in Narration • Writing About Symbols	• Determining Point of View • Having Questions in Mind	• Answering Questions About Details

Chapter	Reading Strategies	Writing Strategies
Chapter 6 **Abnormal Psychology** • Introduction: *Culture and Mental Illness* • General Interest Reading: *What is Abnormal?* • Academic Reading: *Approaches to Psychological Therapy*	• Understanding Connotation • Finding an Implied Main Idea	• Focus: Writing a Summary Paragraph • Strategy: Paraphrasing and Citing Your Sources
UNIT 4 HEALTH		
Chapter 7 **Medicine and Drugs: Addictive Substances** • Introduction: *Consequences of Addiction* • General Interest Reading: *Drug Use and Abuse Worldwide* • Academic Reading: *Addiction: What Can Be Done About It?*	• Understanding Metaphors • Noticing British English	• Focus: Writing a Persuasive Paragraph • Strategy: Writing a Good Proposition
Chapter 8 **The Mind-Body Relationship** • Introduction: *What Does New Research Tell Us?* • General Interest Reading: *The New Science of Mind and Body* • Academic Reading: *A Skeptical Look: Placebo Effect*	• Scanning for Specific Information • Guessing the Meaning from Context: Review of Dictionary Use	• Focus: Writing a Persuasive Paragraph • Strategy: Hedging

The Mechanics of Writing	Critical Thinking Strategies	Test-Taking Strategies
• Passive Voice • Writing Definitions with Adjective Clauses • Writing About Advantages and Disadvantages • Adverbial Conjunctions	• Using a T-Chart to Analyze Advantages and Disadvantages • Finding an Implied Main Idea	• Understanding Stems and Affixes
UNIT 4 HEALTH		
• Subordinating Conjunctions • Identifying and Repairing Fragments • Present Unreal Conditional	• Predicting Opposing Arguments • Understanding Metaphors	• Finding Sentences with Similar Meaning
• Expressing Possibility • Review of Conjunctions • Italics and Quotation Marks	• Seeing Two Sides of an Issue • Hedging	• Determining Topic, Main Point, Purpose, and Tone

UNIT 1 ●●●●● BUSINESS

○ Direct students' attention to the photo on page 1. Ask questions: *Who do you see in the picture? What can you see in the background?*
○ Write *business* on the board and help students brainstorm words related to business. Ask: *What topics do you think will be in this unit?* Circle the words they suggest.

CHAPTER 1 DOING BUSINESS INTERNATIONALLY

In Part 1 of this chapter, students will read about international marketing mistakes related to differences in language and culture. In Part 2, they will read about how cultures differ in language, religion, values and attitudes, customs and manners, and material culture. In Part 3, students will learn about cultural intelligence. Part 4 focuses on the mechanics of writing, including present and past tenses, modals of advice, and adjective clauses. Finally, in Part 5, students will write expository paragraphs about one thing that multinational companies should understand about their cultures.

VOCABULARY

acquire	bow	economics	marketplace	social
adapt	challenge	event	material culture	infrastructure
appropriate	confirm	financial	measure	status
avoid	costly	infrastructure	overlapping	support
behavior	depict	harmony	pursue	technology
boss	economic	hierarchy	risk	work ethic
boundary	infrastructure	ignore	score	

READING STRATEGIES

Understanding New Words
Dealing with New Words
Guessing the Meaning from Context: Punctuation
Finding the Main Idea
Finding Details
Thinking Ahead
Guessing the Meaning from Context: Using Logic
Using Graphic Organizers: Venn Diagrams and Charts

CRITICAL THINKING STRATEGIES

Thinking Ahead (Parts 1, 2, 3)
Making Inferences (Part 1)
Note: The strategy in bold is highlighted in the student book.

MECHANICS

Simple Present and Simple Past
Modals of Advice
The Subject *You*
Adjective Clauses
Transitional Expressions: Coordinating Conjunctions

WRITING STRATEGY

Writing an Expository Paragraph

TEST-TAKING STRATEGIES

Finding Errors
Editing a Test Essay

CHAPTER 1 Doing Business Internationally

Chapter 1 Opener, page 3

❍ Direct students' attention to the chapter title and photo. Discuss the questions with the class.
❍ Ask: *What foreign products are advertised in our area?*

PART 1 INTRODUCTION
INTERNATIONAL MARKETING MISTAKES, PAGES 4–7

PREVIEW ACTIVITY: Sort by Category

❍ Explain the activity. Tell students that you will give them a question to ask classmates. Then they will move around the classroom, asking the question and standing with people who have the same or similar answers to the question.
❍ Ask: *What's your favorite type of restaurant?* Remind students to move around and talk to each other so that they can group themselves according to response. When students are grouped, ask each group what they represent (*Italian, seafood, burgers*).
❍ Ask additional questions related to the topics in the chapter. Create your own or use the ones below. This activity is meant to warm students up to the topics and help them get to know each other.
What kind of shoes do you wear on most days?
What's your favorite commercial on TV?
What product from the U.S. do you use the most?
What is one American custom you think is strange?

Culture Note

❍ Starbucks is a coffee company with stores in countries around the world. It first opened in Seattle, Washington, in 1971. In 2005, Starbucks had nearly 10,000 stores selling coffee drinks, coffee beans, and equipment for making coffee.

Before Reading

CRITICAL THINKING STRATEGY: Thinking Ahead

Thinking ahead is an important critical thinking strategy used throughout the text. By looking at and discussing photos, students can anticipate the content of the reading. Predicting and anticipating content helps students understand new material.

Thinking Ahead

❍ Have students look at the photos and read the questions.
❍ Put students in pairs to discuss the questions.
❍ Call on students to share their ideas with the class.

ANSWER KEY

1. the United States; 2. Spanish and Hebrew; Spain, Mexico, any country in Central or South America, Israel 3. Answers will vary.

EXPANSION ACTIVITY: Foreign Products

❍ Put students in pairs or small groups to brainstorm a list of foreign products sold locally.
❍ Set a time limit of three minutes. Elicit the examples of products and write them on the board.
❍ Ask students for the names of local companies that produce the same products.

🎧 Reading

❍ Have students look at the reading. Read the title and the five headings within the reading. Ask: *How many mistakes will the reading discuss?*
❍ Go over the directions and the question.
❍ Have students read silently, or have students follow along silently as you play the audio program.

Culture Note

❍ Nike is a very famous company that sells athletic shoes and clothing. Its founders, Phil Knight and Bill Bowerman, met in the 1950s and started an athletic shoe company in the 1960s. The shoes got their unusual bottom tread when Bowerman began experimenting by pouring rubber on his wife's waffle iron. Nike was the Greek goddess of victory. The Nike company and the famous logo, a "swoosh," were created in 1971. In 2003, Nike's international sales exceeded its sales in the U.S.

After Reading

A. Check Your Understanding

❍ Go over the directions.
❍ Have students discuss the question in pairs.
❍ Go over the answers with the class.

ANSWER KEY

KFC: The company didn't know about the unfortunate translation of "finger-lickin' good" to "eat your fingers off."
Traficante: The name of the company means "drug dealer" in Spanish.
Samarin: People in Arab countries read from right to left, so it looks like the product makes people sick.
Gerber Baby Food: People in Africa might think babies are in the jars.
Nike: They didn't understand what the Kenyan in the ad was really saying.

CRITICAL THINKING STRATEGY: Making Inferences

❍ Go over the information in the box.
❍ Ask: *When do readers need to make inferences?*

B. Making Inferences

❍ Go over the directions.
❍ Have students make inferences and write their answers in the boxes.
❍ Put students in pairs to check their answers.
❍ Go over the answers with the class.

Grammar Note

❍ Students might not be familiar with the use of *wish* to express an unreal situation (*The company probably wishes that it had asked . . .*). You may want to point out that *wish* is usually used with the simple past or the past perfect, similar to unreal conditionals.

ANSWER KEY

Traficante: People might think drug dealers made it or there were drugs in it. People probably don't want a product that's associated with drug dealers.
Nike: No one in the United States would understand Maa (the Kenyan language).
Samarin: The company didn't ask Arabic speakers about the advertising program first.

TOEFL® iBT Tip

TOEFL iBT Tip 1: The TOEFL iBT tests the examinee's ability to read a text and make inferences based on information presented in the text. For this basic comprehension skill, examinees may be required to form generalizations and draw conclusions based on what is implied in a text.

❍ Point out to students that the strategy for *Making Inferences* will help them to determine what an author means when information is not stated directly.

❍ By using key words and phrases from the text, students will be able to make assumptions and apply this skill to the reading section of the TOEFL iBT.

On the TOEFL iBT, this question may appear in the following formats:
  Which of the following can be inferred from paragraph __ about _____?
  What can be inferred about _____?

READING STRATEGY: Understanding New Words

❍ Go over the information in the box.
❍ Tell students that in this text they will learn many strategies for understanding new words. Encourage students to read without using their dictionaries.

C. Understanding New Words

❍ Go over the directions and questions.
❍ Direct students' attention to the pictures on page 7.
❍ Put students in pairs to answer the questions. Encourage students to guess what the captions could be.
❍ Call on students to share their ideas with the class.

ANSWER KEY

Answers will vary.

EXPANSION ACTIVITY: Ad Analysis

❍ Have students bring in ads from magazines, or bring in ads for students to use.
❍ Ask students to choose several ads that they think might be a problem in a different culture.
❍ Put students in small groups to discuss an ad and how it might be a problem. You may wish to model this first with an ad.
❍ Ask each group to present their ideas to the class.

PART ❷ GENERAL INTEREST READING
INTERNATIONAL CULTURE, PAGES 8–15

Before Reading
A. Thinking Ahead

❍ Go over the directions and the questions.
❍ Put students in small groups to discuss the questions.
❍ Call on students to share their ideas with the class.

Culture Notes

❍ The first picture shows an outdoor marketplace in the Middle East. In most outdoor marketplaces, the buyer and seller discuss and agree upon a price. Outdoor marketplaces are less common in the United States, and the prices are usually set. Buyers and sellers are less likely to bargain in the United States than in other cultures, although at yard sales and flea markets, bargaining does take place.
❍ Bowing in Asian countries shows respect and is a very important cultural custom. People don't bow when they meet or greet others in the United States.
❍ In many Latin American cultures, hitting the elbow indicates that someone is tight or cheap with money.

ANSWER KEY

1. marketplace in the Middle East – shopping; Asia – greeting each other; Latin America – talking
2. Answers will vary. Ideas might include the following: issues around time, small talk, gestures and body language, gifts, understanding values.
3. Answers will vary, but might include the following: when and how people eat, how men and women interact, how to ask for things politely, tipping.

READING STRATEGY: Dealing with New Words

❍ Go over the information in the box.
❍ Ask comprehension questions: *What should you do when you find a word you don't know? Why shouldn't you use a dictionary? When is it hard to guess? How do you know if a word is essential? What kind of dictionary should you use if you must look up a word?*

B. Dealing with New Words

❍ Go over the directions and the first example. Ask for other guesses for the word *ebbist*.
❍ Have students write their answers and then compare ideas with a partner.
❍ Call on students to share their ideas with the class.

ANSWER KEY

Answers may vary.
1. Yes, it is possible to guess the meaning; companies.
2. No, it is not possible to guess the meaning. Yes, the word is important.
3. Yes, it is possible to guess the meaning; mistaken ideas.
4. Yes, it is possible to guess the meaning, but not exactly; institutions, systems, social services.
5. Yes, it is possible to guess the meaning; not said directly, implied.
6. Yes, it is possible to guess the meaning, but not exactly; late or early.

READING STRATEGY: Guessing the Meaning from Context: Punctuation

❍ Go over the information in the box.
❍ Ask: *What punctuation marks often indicate a definition?*
❍ Have students underline or highlight definitions as they read.

C. Guessing the Meaning from Context

❍ Go over the directions.
❍ Have students look for the meanings of new words after commas or dashes, or in parentheses.

🎧 Reading

❍ Go over the directions and the question.
❍ Have students read *International Culture* silently, or have them follow along silently as you play the audio program.
❍ Ask students what definitions they marked in the reading.

ANSWER KEY

A knowledge of culture can help a company adapt its practices and products to another culture.
Students will find definitions for the following terms: *adapt, misconception, Protestant work ethic, technology, economics, social infrastructure,* and *financial infrastructure.*

EXPANSION ACTIVITY: Take Notes

❍ Photocopy and distribute the Black Line Master *Taking Notes on* International Culture on page BLM 1.
❍ Have students complete the graphic organizer and then compare ideas with a partner.
❍ Call on students to share their ideas with the class.

After Reading

READING STRATEGY: Finding the Main Idea

❍ Go over the information in the box.
❍ Ask comprehension questions: *Where do you usually find the introduction in an essay? Where is the conclusion? What is a main idea? Where can we often find it?*

A. Finding the Main Idea

❍ Go over the directions.
❍ Have students review the reading and underline one sentence in the first paragraph and one sentence in the last paragraph that give the main idea.
❍ Put students in pairs to compare answers.
❍ Go over the answers with the class.

ANSWER KEY

First paragraph:
If people want to be successful in global business, they must understand the cultures of other countries and learn how to adapt to them, or change their practices in different cultures.
Last paragraph:
Without an understanding of cultures, global businesses will not be successful.

B. Vocabulary Check

❍ Go over the directions.
❍ Tell students to match the words with the definitions and then to check their answers in pairs.
❍ Go over the answers with the class.

ANSWER KEY

1. e; 2. a; 3. h; 4. d; 5. f; 6. c; 7. g; 8. b

READING STRATEGY: Finding Details

❍ Go over the information in the box.
❍ Ask: *What words can help you find important details?*

C. Finding Details

❍ Go over the directions and the questions.
❍ Have students highlight the answers and then compare ideas with a partner.
❍ Go over the answers with the class.

ANSWER KEY

1. (1)The company uses the same methods abroad that it uses in the home country. (2) It doesn't adapt (change) a product to fit the needs of another country. (3) It sends managers with no international experience to work abroad.
2. A knowledge of the local language can help an international businessperson in four ways. First, the person can communicate directly, without relying on someone else to translate or explain what is happening. Second, people are usually more open in their communication with someone who speaks their language. Third, an understanding of the language allows the person to notice the implied meanings and other information that is not said directly. Finally, knowing the language helps the person to understand the culture better.
3. When we study material culture, we need to think about how people make things (technology) and who makes them and why (economics).

TOEFL® iBT Tip

TOEFL iBT Tip 2: TOEFL iBT tests the ability to understand key facts and the important information contained within a text. Locating details and key words in a text will help students build vocabulary and improve their reading skills.

❍ Point out that the reading section of the TOEFL iBT may require examinees to identify information that is NOT included in the passage.

❍ The *Finding Details* activity helps students locate more than one fact presented in a passage. This will help to scaffold students' abilities upward toward mastering the *negative fact question* on the test.

On the TOEFL iBT, this question may appear in the following formats:
   All of the following are mentioned in paragraph __ as ____ EXCEPT . . .
   According to the passage, which of the following is an example of ____?

CRITICAL THINKING STRATEGY: Making Connections

Making connections is an important critical thinking strategy. By connecting new information to something we know or have read, we are better able to understand, synthesize, and remember.

D. Making Connections

❍ Go over the directions.
❍ Have students identify the elements that each company ignored.
❍ Put students in small groups to compare answers.
❍ Call on students to share their answers with the class.

ANSWER KEY

Answers may vary.
KFC: language; Traficante: values and attitudes, language; Samarin: language (direction of reading); Nike: language; Gerber: customs and manners, material culture

E. Extension

❍ Go over the directions.
❍ Have students answer the questions.
❍ Put students in small groups to discuss their answers.
❍ Direct students' attention to the answers on page 34.
❍ Ask: *What surprised you? How good is your knowledge of customs?*

ANSWERS

1. b	6. c
2. c	7. b
3. b	8. b
4. a	9. c
5. c	10. b

PART ③ ACADEMIC READING
IMPROVING CQ: UNDERSTANDING CULTURAL VALUES, PAGES 16–24

Before Reading
READING STRATEGY: Thinking Ahead
○ Go over the information in the box.
○ Ask comprehension questions: *Why should you think about a topic before reading about it? What should you do as you read? How will this help you?*

A. Thinking Ahead
○ Go over the directions. Read the questions aloud.
○ Give students time to think about their answers.
○ Call on several students to share their answers with the class.

ANSWER KEY
Answers will vary.

B. Taking a Survey
○ Direct students' attention to the chart. You may want to model how to do the activity by asking a few students the question and filling in the chart.
○ Have students stand and move around the classroom to take turns asking and answering the questions. Remind students to talk to five classmates and to write their answers on the chart.
○ Put students in small groups to discuss their charts.
○ Call on students to tell the class what they found out.

ANSWER KEY
Answers will vary.

READING STRATEGY: Guessing the Meaning from Context: Using Logic
○ Go over the information in the box.
○ Ask comprehension questions: *What is logic? What is a strategy you can use to guess the word's meaning?*

C. Vocabulary Preparation
○ Go over the directions.
○ Have students match the definitions with the words and then check their answers with a partner.
○ Go over the answers with the class.

ANSWER KEY *Pg 18 Student Text*
1. g; 2. h; 3. e; 4. c; 5. a; 6. b; 7. d; 8. f

TOEFL® iBT Tip

TOEFL iBT Tip 3: The TOEFL iBT tests the ability to determine the meaning of words in context.

○ Point out that the reading strategy *Guessing the Meaning from Context: Using Logic* will help students improve their vocabulary for the TOEFL iBT. By interpreting a sentence based on other information, and using the logic of grammar, students can figure out the meaning of new words presented in context.

On the TOEFL iBT, vocabulary questions appear in the following format:
The word _____ in the passage is closest in meaning to . . .

EXPANSION ACTIVITY: Original Sentences
○ Have students write their own sentences using the new words.
○ Put students in pairs to read their sentences.
○ Call on students to read their sentences to the class.

🎧 Reading

○ Go over the directions before the reading. Read the questions aloud. Point out that students will have to answer these questions after they read.
○ Have students read the article silently, or play the audio program and have students follow along silently.

After Reading

A. Check Your Understanding

○ Go over the directions.
○ Have students write answers to the questions and then compare ideas with a partner.
○ Call on students to share their ideas with the class.

ANSWER KEY

1. The three components of cultural intelligence are knowledge, behavioral skills, and mindfulness.
2. Most of the reading deals with cultural knowledge.

B. Vocabulary Check

○ Go over the directions.
○ Have students write the correct words on the lines and then check their answers with a partner.
○ Go over the answers with the class.

ANSWER KEY

1. hierarchy; 2. costly; 3. boundaries; 4. pursue;
5. harmony; 6. behavior

EXPANSION ACTIVITY: Vocabulary Notebook

○ Point out that using a vocabulary notebook can help students remember new vocabulary.
○ Have students skim the reading and write down unfamiliar words and what they guess the words mean.
○ Have students confirm the meanings by looking the words up in an English-English dictionary.

READING STRATEGY: Using Graphic Organizers: Venn Diagrams and Charts

○ Go over the information in the box.
○ Elicit the meanings of the words in bold (*visualize, depicted, Venn diagram, chart*).
○ Ask comprehension questions: *Why are graphic organizers helpful? When would you use a Venn diagram? When would you use a chart?*

C. Using Graphic Organizers: Venn Diagrams and Charts

○ Go over the directions.
○ Have students complete the Venn diagram and then compare ideas with a partner.
○ Go over the answers with the class.

ANSWER KEY

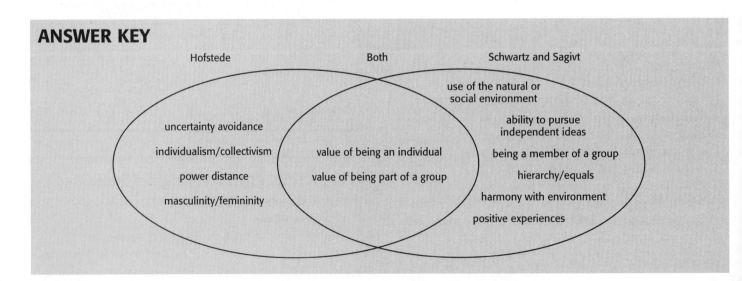

Hofstede

uncertainty avoidance

individualism/collectivism

power distance

masculinity/femininity

Both

value of being an individual

value of being part of a group

Schwartz and Sagivt

use of the natural or social environment

ability to pursue independent ideas

being a member of a group

hierarchy/equals

harmony with environment

positive experiences

┌─────────────────────────────────────┐
│ **TOEFL® iBT Tip** │
└─────────────────────────────────────┘

TOEFL iBT Tip 4: TOEFL iBT tests the ability to understand facts, examples, and explanations in a text; however, it does not directly test understanding of the main idea of a passage.

○ The *Using Graphic Organizers* activity requires students to visually connect information. This will help to scaffold students' abilities upward toward mastering the schematic table questions on the test.

○ Remind students that being able to skim and scan to locate information is a technique that will help them with the schematic table question type on the test.

D. Making Connections

○ Remind students that synthesizing, or combining information from different sources, is an important critical thinking skill.
○ Go over the directions.
○ Put students in pairs to discuss the questions.
○ Call on students to share their ideas with the class.

ANSWER KEY

Answers may vary.
The mistakes were costly because consumers in other countries would be less likely to buy the products. The companies lost business, respect, credibility.

E. Analysis: Cultural Values

○ Go over the directions and the questions.
○ Put students in small groups to discuss the questions.
○ Call on students to share their ideas with the class.

ANSWER KEY

Answers will vary.

F. Application: The Elements of Culture

○ Go over the directions.
○ Have students work individually and take notes on their culture according to the five elements.

G. Discussion

○ Go over the directions.
○ Put students in small groups to share their ideas.
○ Call on students to share their ideas with the class.

H. Response Writing

○ Go over the directions. Explain that this is a quick-writing activity and does not have to be perfect. Point out that response writing can be a warm-up to a more structured writing assignment, helping to generate ideas.
○ Set a time limit of ten minutes.
○ Put students in pairs to read or talk about their writing.

Website Research

○ For additional information on cultural differences, refer students to these websites:
  • Geert Hofstede
    http://www.geert-hofstede.com/
  • Global Edge: Business Etiquette Around the World
    http://globaledge.msu.edu/ibrd/GR_Culture.asp
  • BBC World Service, Learning English: Working Abroad
    http://blue.butler.edu/~jfmcgrat/culture.htm

PART ④ THE MECHANICS OF WRITING, PAGES 25–31

○ Go over the information about Part 4.

┌─────────────────────────────────────┐
│ **TOEFL® iBT Tip** │
└─────────────────────────────────────┘

TOEFL iBT Tip 5: Although the TOEFL iBT does not discretely test grammar skills, examinees' essay scores will be determined based on the range of grammar and vocabulary used in their essays.

○ Point out that the grammar activities in *The Mechanics of Writing* part of this chapter will help them improve their use of verb tenses, as well as adjectives and conjunctions for essay writing.

TOEFL iBT essays may be scored higher based on whether or not the examinee can use verb tenses, such as the simple present and simple past, or modals of advice correctly in a sentence. Using correct grammar and more sophisticated phrases will help students improve their overall essay writing abilities and their scores on the test.

Simple Present and Simple Past

○ Go over the information in the box about the simple present and the simple past.
○ Ask questions: *When do we use the simple present? How do we form the third person singular? How do we make a negative in the simple present? When do we use the simple past?*

A. Simple Present and Simple Past

○ Go over the directions.
○ Have students complete the sentences with the correct form of the verb in parentheses.
○ Go over the answers with the class.

ANSWER KEY

1. does; 2. needs; 3. have; 4. means; 5. receive; 6. is; 7. don't have; 8. opened; 9. were not; 10. were; 11. followed; 12. treated; 13. didn't appreciate; 14. complained; 15. didn't understand; 16. didn't do; 17. felt; 18. took; 19. won; 20. had

Modals of Advice

○ Go over the information in the box.
○ Ask: *What expressions do we use to give advice? What form of the modals do we use for advice in the past? What form of the main verb follows modals?*

Grammar Notes

○ You may want to remind students that *ought to* is not like a modal in form, but we often use the expression in the same way we use the modal *should*.
○ We often use the expressions *should have* + past participle and *ought to have* + past participle to express a regret about what was or was not done.

B. Modals of Advice

○ Go over the directions and the example.
○ Direct students' attention to the second prompt (*shake hands when you say "hello" or "good-bye"/ Italy*) and elicit the correct advice (*In Italy, you should shake hands when you say "hello" or "good-bye."*)
○ Put students in pairs to take turns giving advice to George using the prompts.
○ Ask students questions: *What should George do in Japan? What shouldn't he do in France?*

ANSWER KEY

1. You ought to/should flatter your host in Taiwan.
2. You ought to/should shake hands when you say "hello" or "good-bye" in Italy.
3. You ought to/should learn how to bow in Japan.
4. You ought to/should touch your left fingers to your right arm when giving or receiving something in Korea.
5. You ought to/should use the spoon above the plate for dessert in Greece.
6. You shouldn't refuse a drink in Russia.
7. You shouldn't give an even number of flowers in France.
8. You shouldn't eat with your fingers in Turkey.
9. You shouldn't use the American hand signal for okay in Brazil.
10. You shouldn't have three people in a photograph in Vietnam.

C. Modals

○ Go over the directions.
○ Model the activity. Read the example for Activity B. Elicit the advice about the past (*You should have flattered your host in Taiwan*).
○ If your students need more written practice with past modals, have students write the sentences from Activity B using the past form.
○ Put students in pairs to take turns giving advice about the past using the prompts in Activity B.
○ Call on students and ask questions: *What mistake did George make in Italy?*

EXPANSION ACTIVITY: Personal Experience

❍ Model the activity. Describe an experience you had traveling when you made mistakes (*I went to Mexico last year. I should have been more careful buying food at the outdoor markets. I shouldn't have bought so many big gifts to bring home. I ought to have studied more Spanish before I went*).

❍ Have students write a paragraph about an experience they had traveling where they made mistakes. Remind students to use *should have/ought to have/shouldn't have* + past participle to describe their mistakes.

❍ Put students in pairs to read their paragraphs.

❍ Call on students to read their paragraphs to the class.

The Subject *You*

❍ Go over the information in the box.

❍ Ask comprehension questions: *What are two pronouns we can use to talk about people in general? Which pronoun is more formal?*

D. Application

❍ Go over the directions.

❍ Have students write five sentences with advice for people who travel to their countries. Remind students to use *should(n't)* or *ought to* and to begin each sentence with *you*.

❍ Put students in small groups to share their sentences.

❍ Call on students to read their sentences to the class. Have students select the most important advice out of the five sentences read.

ANSWER KEY

Answers will vary.

Adjective Clauses

❍ Go over the information in the box.

❍ Ask comprehension questions: *What does an adjective clause do? Where do we put adjective clauses? What words often begin adjective clauses? When do we use commas?*

Grammar Notes

❍ Your students may have learned that the words that introduce adjective clauses (*who, that, which, where, whose*) are often called relative pronouns.

❍ It may be helpful to explain that an adjective clause often answers the question: *Which one?* If the information in the adjective clause is necessary to answer *which one*, then we don't use commas. For example, in the sentence *The woman who answered the door wore a red dress*, we need the information in the adjective clause to understand which woman we are talking about. However, in the sentence *Pope John Paul II, who died in 2005, was succeeded by Pope Benedict XVI*, we don't need the information to know who we are talking about, so we use commas.

❍ Your students may know that sometimes a relative pronoun is not used. Although they will not practice that type of clause in this chapter, you may explain that we don't use a relative pronoun when the noun is the object of the adjective clause (*The class I took last year was very interesting*).

E. Adjective Clauses

❍ Go over the directions.

❍ Have students underline the adjective clauses and draw arrows to the nouns they modify.

❍ Put students in pairs to check their answers.

❍ Go over the answers with the class.

ANSWER KEY

1. The first question that an American usually asks a new acquaintance is "What do you do?"

2. A woman who is traveling in the Middle East should not wear short skirts or low-cut blouses.

3. He spent time in three countries where his company did business.

4. In Arab countries, when a man greets another man who has higher status, he should wait until the other man offers to shake hands.

5. Customs that are very different in various cultures involve the use of gestures—hand movements for communication.

CHAPTER 1 • Doing Business Internationally **• 11**

F. Sentence Combining: Adjective Clauses

- ❍ Go over the directions and the example.
- ❍ Have students combine the pairs of sentences. Remind students to make the second sentence the adjective clause.
- ❍ Have students check their answers with a partner.
- ❍ Go over the answers with the class.

ANSWER KEY

1. A business that is culturally insensitive will probably not be successful.
2. The woman who called the meeting was the new manager.
3. One custom that seems a little unusual to some people is going to public baths.
4. We visited an acquaintance whose home was just outside the city.
5. An American who crosses his fingers is saying "Good luck."
6. Kevin went to work for a company that did a lot of international business.

Transitional Expressions: Coordinating Conjunctions

- ❍ Go over the information in the box.
- ❍ Ask comprehension questions: *What is an independent clause? Which conjunction would you use to say* because? *What does* so *mean? Which conjunction sometimes introduces unexpected information? When do we use commas with conjunctions?*

Grammar Notes

- ❍ Some students find the mnemonic FANBOYS (*for, and, nor, but, or, yet, so*) helps them remember the coordinating conjunctions.
- ❍ You may want to point out that the coordinating conjunction *for* is seldom used, especially in conversation.
- ❍ Note that in some writing styles, the serial comma is not used before *and* or *or.* The Associate Press does not use the final comma.

G. Sentence Combining: Coordinating Conjunctions

- ❍ Go over the directions.
- ❍ Read the first pair of sentences and elicit what conjunctions should be used and why.
- ❍ Have students combine the sentences.
- ❍ Have students check their answers with a partner.
- ❍ Go over the answers with the class.

ANSWER KEY

1. She had lived in Finland for 15 years, so she spoke the language fluently.
2. It's a good idea to bring a gift to the hostess, but/yet you shouldn't bring a really expensive gift the first time you visit.
3. The company produces cars, trucks, and vans.
4. You need to ask for the bill in a restaurant in Italy, or the waiter won't bring it.
5. In Spain, an older person may use your first name, but/yet you should use an older person's last name.
6. You may have tea, juice, and/or water.
7. The company wasn't successful, for it didn't understand the business customs of the country.
8. Most people in that country speak two languages, but/yet/and some speak three or four.

H. Finding Errors

- ❍ Go over the directions.
- ❍ Direct students' attention to the first item and elicit the letter of the section that contains the error (A). Ask students why the comma is not needed (the adjective clause has essential information).
- ❍ Have students circle the letters of the errors and then compare answers with a partner.
- ❍ Go over the answers with the class. Have students explain what the errors are and how to correct them.

ANSWER KEY

1. A; 2. C; 3. B; 4. C; 5. B

EXPANSION ACTIVITY: Editing Practice
○ Photocopy and distribute the Black Line Master *Editing Practice* on page BLM 2.
○ Go over the directions.
○ Have students correct the mistakes and then compare answers with a partner.
○ Go over the answers with the class.

ANSWER KEY

U.S. companies/ that do business in Japan should ~~to~~ learn about the culture and language, ^{or} ~~and~~ ∧ they will make the same mistakes others have made. For example, one company trie^ds ∧ to sell a cake mix/ that could be made in a Japanese rice cooker. No one bought it. The company didn't know that Japanese people only want to cook rice in a rice cooker. In Japan, steering wheels are usually on the right side of the car ∧, but when some Japanese buy foreign cars, they want the steering wheel on the left. The left-side steering wheel is higher status. In some parts of Europe, a *taverna* is a place to eat and drink. In Japanese, the word *taberna* mean^ss ∧ "do not eat." Knowing about Japanese culture and language can help U.S. companies avoid costly mistakes.

WRITING STRATEGY: Writing an Expository Paragraph
○ Go over the information in the box.
○ Ask comprehension questions: *What three things are included in an expository paragraph? What is one type of specific evidence? Why do we include an example? What tense do we use to talk about something that is generally true? How should you end the paragraph?*
○ You may want to read the example paragraph aloud as students follow silently in their books.
○ Go over the points for students to notice in the example, and have them find each of the elements in the paragraph.
○ Read the *Analysis* directions. Ask students to highlight the coordinating conjunctions and adjective clauses in the example.
○ Go over the answers with the class.

ANSWER KEY
Coordinating conjunctions:
They were all smiling and looked friendly, <u>yet</u> there was one problem.
The company ignored the majority of the U.S. population, <u>so</u> the majority of the U.S. population ignored the company and didn't buy the car.
Adjective clauses:
Multinational companies <u>that do business in the United States</u> shouldn't ignore the importance of diversity in U.S. culture.
A business <u>that ignores this</u> is probably making a cultural mistake.

PART 5 ACADEMIC WRITING
PAGES 32–34

Writing Assignment
○ Go over the writing assignment.
○ Have students read Steps A–F on pages 32–34. Explain that they will always follow these steps for writing their paragraphs.
○ Direct students' attention to Step A and have students choose one element of culture to write about.
○ Direct students' attention to Step B. Have students choose one example of this element from their notes on page 24.

TOEFL® iBT Tip

TOEFL iBT Tip 6: Both the integrated and independent essays of the TOEFL iBT are scored based on how well the examinee completes the overall writing task. Many of the reading passages, as well as the writing tasks, involve expository essay format.

○ Point out that the *Writing an Expository Paragraph* activities will help students improve their coherence and linking the flow of ideas in their essays. It will help them to build their point of view and develop reasons and evidence to support their opinions.

CRITICAL THINKING STRATEGY: Synthesizing

Synthesizing—combining and unifying ideas in a new way—is an important critical thinking strategy. In this writing assignment, students must formulate points of view and select reasons and evidence to support their opinions. To do this, students will need to synthesize what they have read and learned in this chapter.

○ Direct students' attention to Step C. Go over the three suggestions to plan their paragraphs. You may wish to model the steps for students by writing a topic on the board, listing ideas, and then editing the list. Use the Black Line Master in the Expansion Activity below. As students work on Step C, walk around the room and offer help as needed.

EXPANSION ACTIVITY: Outline a Paragraph

○ Photocopy and distribute the Black Line Master *Outlining a Paragraph of Analysis* on page BLM 3.
○ Go over the directions.
○ After students have done Step C, have them fill in the outline to organize their ideas. When they finish, they can use their outlines as they write their paragraphs.

○ Direct students' attention to Step D. Have students write paragraphs, using the notes in Step C. Point

out that in this step, the most important thing is to write out their ideas. They will edit and revise in the next step.

TEST-TAKING STRATEGY: Editing a Test Essay
○ Go over the information with students.
○ Ask questions such as: *Have you taken an essay test? How much time did you have to write your answer? How much time did you spend checking your writing before handing in your test?*

○ Go over the list of editing questions in Step E. Have students read and edit their paragraphs, using the questions as a guide. You may wish to have students circle or underline the elements in their paragraphs.
○ For peer editing, have students exchange paragraphs with a partner, edit, and return the paper to the writer. Some students may find peer editing challenging at first. Explain to students that it is a good way to improve editing skills. It is also easier to see errors in someone else's writing, so it is helpful to have someone else check your writing. With practice, students will become more comfortable with checking a classmate's paragraph.
○ Go over the directions for Step F. Have students carefully rewrite their paragraphs and hand them in to you.
○ After you have read and returned students' paragraphs, you may want to set aside time for students to read each other's writing or display the paragraphs in the classroom. Have students keep all of their final versions in a notebook or folder so that they can see their progress and improvement over time.

EXPANSION ACTIVITY: Presentations
○ Put students in small groups according to the element of culture that they chose to focus on.
○ Have students in each group share the information that they wrote about in their paragraphs.
○ Instruct each small group to prepare a three to five minute presentation on that element of culture, using the examples they wrote about. You may want to give students time to research the topic a little more.
○ Have the groups present to the class.

UNIT 1 ●○○○○● BUSINESS

CHAPTER 2 THE GLOBAL ECONOMY

In Part 1, students will first read about how supply and demand operates in different cultures. In Part 2, students will read about an Englishman's attempt to buy a house on the island of Cyprus (with the help of a clever Turkish real estate agent). In Part 3, students will learn about different economic systems. Part 4 focuses on the mechanics of writing, including the passive voice, adverbial conjunctions, and avoiding and repairing run-ons and comma splices. Finally, in Part 5, students will write a paragraph in which they analyze the economic system of the country they were born in or live in now.

VOCABULARY

bang	domesticated	last	rotten
bribe	economist	market economy	safe
capitalism	edible	mixed economy	sip
command economy	false	nomadic	supply
controlled	gatherer	note	swear
crop	goods	potlatch	tend
delicately	herd	prairie dog	timber
demand	hunter	reciprocal	tribal
determine	intervene	regulate	
distribution	labor	resource	

READING STRATEGIES
Previewing for Topics
Guessing the Meaning from Context: Accepting
    Incomplete Knowledge
Understanding Parts of Speech
Keeping a Word Journal
Guessing the Meaning from Context: Using the
    Next Sentence
Marking a Textbook
Finding the Topic Sentence
Using Graphic Organizers: Charts

CRITICAL THINKING STRATEGIES
Thinking Ahead (Parts 1, 2, and 3)
Synthesizing and Applying Information (Part 3)
Analysis (Part 5)
Note: The strategy in bold is highlighted in the
    student book.

MECHANICS
The Passive Voice
Transitional Expressions: Adverbial Conjunctions
Recognizing and Repairing Run-ons and Comma
    Splices

WRITING STRATEGIES
Writing a Topic Sentence
Writing a Paragraph of Analysis

TEST-TAKING STRATEGY
Guessing the Meaning from Context

CHAPTER 2   The Global Economy

Chapter 2 Opener, page 35

○ Direct students' attention to the photo and questions. Read the questions aloud.
○ Put students in pairs to discuss the questions.
○ Call on students to share their ideas with the class.

PART 1 INTRODUCTION
THE EXCHANGE OF MATERIAL GOODS, PAGES 36–39

Before Reading

A. Thinking Ahead

○ Have students look at the photo on page 36.
○ Go over the directions and the questions.
○ Put students in pairs to discuss the questions.
○ Call on students to share their ideas with the class.

ANSWER KEY

Answers will vary.

EXPANSION ACTIVITY: Top Five

○ Put students in small groups.
○ Have each group come up with a list of the five most popular toys or the top five electronic gadgets. Each group can decide what type of list to make.
○ Have groups decide which items on their lists will be popular in three years and give reasons.
○ Call on representatives from each group to share their ideas with the class.

READING STRATEGY: Previewing for Topics

○ Go over the information in the box.
○ Ask comprehension questions: *What is a topic? What should you do when you preview? What is a caption? What are headings?*

B. Previewing for Topics

○ Go over the directions.
○ Have students preview the reading and write the topics on the lines.
○ Put students in pairs to compare answers.
○ Call on students to share their answers with the class.

ANSWER KEY

1. A North Pacific Coast Ceremony (potlatch)
2. Reindeer Herding
3. Prairie Dogs in the International Economy

🎧 Reading

○ Go over the directions and the question.
○ Have students read the article silently, or have students follow along silently as you play the audio program.

CRITICAL THINKING STRATEGY: Making Connections

Making connections is an important critical thinking strategy. Explain to students that when we connect with a topic, or relate it to something we already know, we comprehend it better and remember it longer.

EXPANSION ACTIVITY: Connect with the Topic

○ Write these questions on the board: *What does this reading remind me of? How do I feel about this?*
○ After reading each of the three subheadings, have students stop and jot down ideas in answer to the two questions. You may wish to model this by putting your own ideas on the board.
○ Put students in pairs or small groups to share their ideas.

💻 Culture Notes

○ Students can get information about, and pictures of, the potlatch ceremony at the following websites:
  • Harvard University's Peabody Museum
    http://www.peabody.harvard.edu/potlatch/
    default.html
  • British Columbia's Heritage
    http://collections.ic.gc.ca/potlatch/.
○ Students can find information about the Sami people of northern Europe at the following websites:
  • University of Texas
    http://www.utexas.edu/courses/sami/
  • University of Connecticut
    http://arcticcircle.uconn.edu/HistoryCulture/
    samiindex.html.
○ Gay Balfour got the idea for the prairie dog vacuum in 1998. He and Dave Honaker are partners in a company called Dog-Gone that rids farmers of prairie dogs using the vacuum. Some animal rights organizations have protested this practice.

After Reading

EXPANSION ACTIVITY: Main Idea

○ Explain that a main idea can be seen as a one-sentence summary of a reading passage.
○ Have students write one-sentence summaries of the article and then compare ideas with a partner.
○ Call on students to share their ideas with the class.

A. Check Your Understanding

○ Go over the directions.
○ Have students discuss the questions in pairs.
○ Go over the answers with the class.

ANSWER KEY

1. The hosts gave away valuable items to their guests.
2. Reindeer provided meat, bones for jewelry, and skins for boots, hats, and other clothing.
3. They had everything they needed.
4. prairie dogs
5. a very large vacuum cleaner
6. Farmers pay him to get rid of the prairie dogs, and people in Tokyo buy the prairie dogs for pets.

TOEFL® iBT Tip

TOEFL iBT Tip 1: The TOEFL iBT tests the ability to understand key facts and the important information contained within a text. Locating key information in a text and discussing that information will help students improve their overall reading and speaking skills in preparation for the Integrated Speaking tasks.

○ Point out that *Check Your Understanding* requires students to discuss their answers with other students, which will help them synthesize information and practice their speaking skills for the integrated speaking questions on the test.

B. Application

○ Go over the directions.
○ Have students write their answers in the chart and then compare ideas with a partner.
○ Go over the answers with the class.

ANSWER KEY

People	Sold or Gave Away	Received
People of the North Pacific Coast	Blankets, food, boats, large pieces of copper	High status
The Samis	Reindeer meat	Snowmobiles
Farmers	Money	No more prairie dogs
People in Tokyo		Prairie dogs as pets

EXPANSION ACTIVITY: Research

❍ Have students use their favorite Internet search engines to find out about an unusual invention.
❍ Call on students to share what they learned with the class.

PART ❷ GENERAL INTEREST READING
BUSINESS IN LITERATURE: DURRELL'S *BITTER LEMONS,* PAGES 40–46

Before Reading
Thinking Ahead
❍ Go over the directions and the questions.
❍ Have students work in small groups to discuss the questions.
❍ Call on students to share their ideas with the class.

Culture Notes
❍ In the United States, people often use real estate agents to help them buy and sell property. Sometimes, a seller will sell a house on his or her own. The seller usually advertises his or her willingness to sell by putting a sign in front of the house and/or an ad in the newspaper or online. Then a potential buyer can contact the seller directly.
❍ In the United States, people don't usually negotiate the price of an item in a store. However, people will often negotiate at a flea market, a yard sale, online, or when buying a car.
❍ Cyprus is an island between Turkey and Greece. The people of Cyprus are called Cypriots. There are Greek Cypriots and Turkish Cypriots.

READING STRATEGY: Guessing the Meaning from Context: Accepting Incomplete Knowledge
❍ Go over the information in the box.

❍ Ask comprehension questions: *Do you always need to know the exact meaning of a word? When is it okay to not worry about the meaning of a particular word? When do you need a dictionary?*

Reading
❍ Go over the directions. You may want to have students highlight new words as they read.
❍ Have students read the excerpt from *Bitter Lemons* silently, or have them follow along silently as you play the audio program.

EXPANSION ACTIVITY: Word Work
❍ Have students write guesses next to unfamiliar words and highlight words they think are important and can't figure out.

After Reading
A. Making Inferences
❍ Go over the directions.
❍ Put students in small groups to discuss the questions.
❍ Call on students to share their ideas with the class.

ANSWER KEY
1. Sabri; 2. The wood is rotten, and they don't want the house. 3. The sentences are in the paragraph that starts on line 35 and in the paragraph that begins on line 58. 4. Answers will vary, but students might anticipate that the woman will sell for the lower price.

EXPANSION ACTIVITY: Role Play
❍ Put students in groups of three and assign each a role from the story (Durrell, Sabri, and the woman).
❍ Have students act out the story in their small groups. Encourage students to enact the emotions from the story.
❍ Ask for volunteers to perform the story for the class.

READING STRATEGY: Understanding Parts of Speech

○ Go over the information in the box.
○ Ask comprehension questions: *What are examples of parts of speech? How can knowing the part of speech help you when you use a dictionary?*

B. Parts of Speech

○ Go over the directions.
○ Have students write the parts of speech and then look the words up in a monolingual dictionary and write the definitions.
○ Have students compare their answers with a partner.
○ Go over the answers with the class.

ANSWER KEY

Definitions will vary.
1. verb, to make a loud noise; 2. noun, a very loud noise; 3. verb, exist, continue; 4. adjective, final; 5. noun, a strong metal box for keeping money; 6. adjective, not in danger; 7. noun, paper money

TOEFL® iBT Tip

TOEFL iBT Tip 2: The TOEFL iBT measures the ability to understand specific words and phrases selected by the author and used in the passage.

○ Point out that the strategy for *Understanding Parts of Speech* and its activity will help students improve their vocabulary for the TOEFL iBT. Understanding grammar in context, and using logic to determine the meaning of unfamiliar vocabulary words will help students build vocabulary and improve their overall comprehension.

TEST-TAKING STRATEGY: Guessing the Meaning from Context

○ Go over the information in the box.
○ Ask: *What is one type of question that you may find on a standardized test? If the test is on a computer, how can you select the answer? Have you ever taken a test on a computer?*

C. Vocabulary Check

○ Go over the directions.
○ Have students write the answers and then compare ideas with a partner.
○ Go over the answers with the class.

ANSWER KEY

1. sipping; 2. floated; 3. timber; 4. delicately; 5. rotten; 6. swear; 7. false; 8. edible

READING STRATEGY: Keeping a Word Journal

○ Go over the information in the box.
○ Ask questions: *What is a Word Journal? How can it help you? What should you include?*
○ You may want to periodically check students' Word Journals to make sure they are adding to them.

D. Word Journal

○ Go over the directions.
○ Have students add new words to their Word Journals.
○ Put students in pairs to talk about the words they selected.

EXPANSION ACTIVITY: Make It Visual

○ Remind students that there are different learning styles, and representing words visually may at least help students remember words better.
○ For each word that students wrote in their Word Journals, have students draw a simple picture or icon to remind them of the word's meaning.
○ Put students in pairs to share their ideas.
○ You may wish to display some of the more artistic or imaginative illustrations in the classroom.
○ This activity will also work well with the expressions in Activity E, *Vocabulary Expansion.*

E. Vocabulary Expansion
❍ Go over the directions.
❍ Have students find the other two expressions
(*as thick as a honeycomb, as thick as salami*)
and compare answers with a partner.
❍ Have students complete the chart for themselves
and then ask two other classmates for their answers.
You may want to put students in groups of three
to complete this activity.

ANSWER KEY
Answers will vary. Remind students to turn to page 64
to find the expressions that are used in the United States.

EXPANSION ACTIVITY: Write It Out
❍ Have students look at the English expressions
on page 46.
❍ Ask students to choose one expression (*busy as a
bee*) as a writing prompt. They should write
a paragraph in which they use the expression
to describe a person or a situation.
❍ Put students in pairs to read their paragraphs.
❍ Call on students to read their paragraphs to the class.

EXPANSION ACTIVITY: Act It Out
❍ Explain the activity. Students will act out scenes
in which one character could be described by one
of the expressions on page 46.
❍ Put students in pairs or groups of three to create
a conversation. Remind students that they should
not use a comparison expression, but they should
create a character or action that could be described
by one of the expressions.
❍ Have the students act out their conversations
in front of the class. Elicit the comparison expression
from the class (*That test was as easy as pie*).

PART ③ ACADEMIC READING
ECONOMIC SYSTEMS, PAGES 47–54

Before Reading
A. Thinking Ahead
❍ Go over the directions. Read the questions aloud.
❍ Put students in small groups to discuss the questions.
❍ Call on students to share their ideas with the class.

ANSWER KEY
Answers will vary.

READING STRATEGY: Guessing the Meaning from Context: Using the Next Sentence
❍ Go over the information in the box.
❍ Ask comprehension questions: *Where is one place
you can look to try to guess the meaning of a word?*

TOEFL® iBT Tip

TOEFL iBT Tip 3: The TOEFL iBT tests the ability
to determine the meanings of words in context.

❍ Point out that the strategy, *Guessing the Meaning
from Context: Using the Next Sentence,* will help
students improve their vocabulary for the TOEFL
iBT. By identifying words that are in *apposition*
to other words and understanding their meanings,
students will be able to apply this information
toward further understanding the concepts
presented in the text.

On the TOEFL iBT, this question appears in the
following format:
The word _____ *in the passage is closest
in meaning to . . .*

B. Vocabulary Preparation
- ❍ Go over the directions.
- ❍ Have students write the part of speech of each word in green on the line and highlight the meaning in the second sentence.
- ❍ Have students check their answers with a partner.
- ❍ Go over the answers with the class.

ANSWER KEY
1. decide; verb
2. oil, minerals, and timber; noun
3. gave out; noun
4. stepped in; verb
5. travelers who move from one area to another to hunt animals and gather fruits and vegetables; adjective + noun.

EXPANSION ACTIVITY: Word Families
- ❍ Write the new words from Activity B on the board. Point out that these words belong to word families, that is, groups of words that have the same base.
- ❍ Elicit words that have *determine* as the base word (*determination, determiner*).
- ❍ Have students work in pairs to generate word families for the other words. You may want to have students use dictionaries if they have a hard time thinking of words.
- ❍ Have volunteers write word families on the board.

C. Previewing
- ❍ Go over the directions.
- ❍ Have students write the topics on the lines and then compare answers with a partner.
- ❍ Go over the answers with the class.

ANSWER KEY
1. Traditional System; 2. Command System; 3. Market System; 4. Mixed System

READING STRATEGY: Marking a Textbook
- ❍ Go over the information in the box.
- ❍ Ask questions: *Why should you mark a book? How should you do this? Why should you use different colors?*

D. Marking a Textbook
- ❍ Go over the directions.
- ❍ Put students in small groups to discuss the questions.
- ❍ If students do not mark in their books, discuss alternatives to using this strategy, such as using a pencil.

ANSWER KEY
Answers will vary.

READING STRATEGY: Finding the Topic Sentence
- ❍ Go over the information in the box.
- ❍ Ask: *What is a topic sentence? Where can you often find it?*

🎧 Reading
- ❍ Go over the directions before the reading. Point out that students will highlight the topic sentence of each paragraph and characteristics of the four economic systems as they read.
- ❍ Have students read *Economic Systems* silently, or play the audio program and have students follow along silently.

Pronunciation Notes: The Effect of the –ic Ending on Word Stress

○ This reading, *Economic Systems*, has several adjectives that end in *–ic* (*economic, nomadic, characteristic*). Point out that this ending can cause a shift in the stress pattern of the word to the syllable just before the ending. For example, in the word *economy*, the primary stress is on the second syllable. However, in *economic*, the primary stress is on the third syllable.

○ Say the words *economy* and *economic* and ask students to repeat. Continue with *nomad, nomadic* and *character, characteristic*.

READING STRATEGY: Using Graphic Organizers: Charts

○ Go over the information in the box.
○ Ask questions: *Why should you use graphic organizers? What would you include on a graphic organizer?*

B. Using Graphic Organizers: Charts

○ Go over the directions.
○ Have students complete the chart and then compare ideas with a partner.
○ Go over the answers with the class. You may want to have students recreate the chart on the board.

After Reading

A. Check Your Understanding

○ Go over the directions. For this activity, have students label the paragraphs with letters, starting with A and ending with F.
○ Put students in small groups to discuss the questions.
○ Call on students to share their ideas with the class.

ANSWER KEY

A. Economists have identified four types of economic systems: traditional, command (or controlled), market (or capitalist), and mixed.
B. A pure traditional economic system answers the four basic questions according to tradition.
C. The government controls production and makes all decisions about the use of goods and services.
D. The opposite of a pure command economic system is a pure market economic system—or capitalism—in which the government does not intervene.
F. A mixed economy has some characteristics of a command economy and some of a market economy.

ANSWER KEY

System	Definitions/Characteristics	Example
Traditional	Economic decisions are based on customs, beliefs, and religion.	the San people
Command	The government controls production and makes all decisions about use of goods and services.	North Korea and Syria
Market	Individual people own the factors of production; the government doesn't intervene.	
Mixed	Most economies are mixed, with some characteristics of a command economy and some characteristics of a market economy.	The United States and China

EXPANSION ACTIVITY: Survey the Book
❍ Have students look through the book to identify different types of graphic organizers.
❍ Elicit types of graphic organizers from the class. You may want to put schematics of the different types on the board (T-chart, mind-map or cluster diagram, Venn diagram, flow chart).

TOEFL® iBT Tip

TOEFL iBT Tip 4: The TOEFL iBT tests the ability to understand facts, examples, and explanations in a text; however, it does not directly test understanding of the main idea of a passage.

❍ The *Using Graphic Organizers* activity requires students to visually connect information. This will help to scaffold students' abilities upward toward mastering the schematic table questions on the test.

❍ Remind students that being able to skim and scan to locate information is a technique that will help them with the schematic table question type on the test.

Students will also benefit from the critical thinking strategy on page 52, which helps them deal with synthesizing and applying the information that they've read. This will aid them in preparation for the Integrated Speaking and Integrated Writing tasks on the test.

C. Vocabulary Check: Words in Economics
❍ Go over the directions.
❍ Have students write the correct words on the lines and then check their answers with a partner.
❍ Go over the answers with the class.

ANSWER KEY
1. economists; 2. controlled economy; 3. capitalism;
4. trade; 5. labor; 6. exchanges; 7. bribe; 8. tends

EXPANSION ACTIVITY: Word Families
❍ Put students in pairs to create word families for the words in Activity C and add them to their Word Journals.

ANSWER KEY
economists, economics, economy, economical, economically
controlled, controllable, controllably
capitalism, capitalist, capital, capitally
trade, trader
labor, laborious
exchange, exchangeable
bribe, bribery
tend, tendency

D. Discussion
❍ Go over the directions.
❍ Put students in small groups to discuss the questions. For variation, assign one question to each group.
❍ Call on students to share their ideas with the class.

ANSWER KEY
Answers will vary.

CRITICAL THINKING STRATEGY: Synthesizing and Applying Information
❍ Go over the information in the box.
❍ Ask questions: *What does* synthesize *mean? What does* apply *mean? How do you think this strategy will help you?*

E. Making Connections
❍ Go over the directions.
❍ Have students complete the chart and then compare answers with a partner.
❍ Call on students to share their ideas with the class.

ANSWER KEY

People	Economic System
People of the North Pacific Coast	Traditional: Potlatch was a custom.
Sami Reindeer Herders	Mixed: The Sami sold their reindeer, but the government regulated the prices.
The Man who Vacuumed Prairie Dogs	Market: He sold his services and the prairie dogs. There's no evidence of government control.
Sabri and the Greek Woman (Part 2)	Traditional: The house was sold using tradition of negotiation.

F. Application: Gathering Information

○ Go over the directions.
○ Have students answer the questionnaire.
○ Put students in pairs to share and compare their answers.
○ Call on students to share their ideas with the class.

ANSWER KEY

Answers will vary.

G. Word Journal

○ Go over the directions.
○ Have students write words in their Word Journals. Encourage students to add word families.

H. Response Writing

○ Go over the directions.
○ Explain that this is a quick-writing activity and does not have to be perfect. Point out that response writing can be a warm-up to a more structured writing assignment, helping to generate ideas.

○ While students are writing, circulate and encourage students to keep writing; suggest that they include examples.
○ Put students in pairs to read or talk about their writing.

Website Research

○ For additional information on economic systems, refer students to these websites:
  • WebEc Economic Systems
    http://www.helsinki.fi/WebEc/webecp.html
  • Wikipedia: Capitalism
    http://en.wikipedia.org/wiki/Capitalism

PART ④ THE MECHANICS OF WRITING, PAGES 55–59

○ Read through the introduction to Part 4 with students.

TOEFL® iBT Tip

TOEFL iBT Tip 5: Although the TOEFL iBT does not discretely test grammar skills, examinees' essay scores are determined based on the range of grammar and vocabulary used in their essays.

○ Point out that the grammar activities in *The Mechanics of Writing* part of this chapter will help them improve their use of the passive voice as well as adverbial conjunctions and transitions for essay writing.

○ TOEFL iBT essays may be scored higher based on whether or not the examinee can use grammar and punctuation correctly in their essays. Using more advanced grammatical structures as well as more sophisticated phrases will help students improve their overall essay writing.

The Passive Voice
○ Go over the information in the box about the passive voice.
○ Ask comprehension questions: *When do we use the passive voice? What happens to the object of the verb when we move from active to passive voice? How is the passive voice formed?*

Grammar Note
○ You may want to point out that we cannot use the passive voice unless there is an object of the verb. For example, in the sentence *He ran very fast*, we cannot use the passive voice because there is no object of the verb *ran*.

A. The Passive Voice
○ Go over the directions.
○ Have students rewrite the sentences.
○ Go over the answers with the class.

ANSWER KEY
1. Economic decisions are based on tradition.
2. Oil was exchanged for wheat.
3. A lot of natural resources will be needed.
4. He may be offered a job.
5. Economic decisions are made in the market.
6. Things are done the way they have always been done.

EXPANSION ACTIVITY: Find Examples
○ Have students find and underline examples of the passive voice in *Economic Systems*.
○ Elicit the examples and write them on the board.

ANSWER KEY
are done; have always been done; are based; will be used; are made; is referred to; is based; is not considered; are supported; are referred to

Transitional Expressions: Adverbial Conjunctions
○ Go over the information in the box.
○ Ask: *What do transitional expressions do? What is an adverbial conjunction? What is an independent clause? What are some types of adverbial conjunctions?*

Grammar Notes
○ Point out that when these expressions are used after a semicolon, they are not capitalized. When they are used at the beginning of a sentence, the expressions begin with a capital letter.
○ Make sure students notice that *then* is an exception to the comma rule. It is the only expression that does not need to be followed by a comma.

B. Sentence Combining: Adverbial Conjunctions
○ Go over the directions.
○ Have students combine the sentences and then compare ideas with a partner. For variation, have students do the activity in pairs.
○ Ask for volunteers to write the sentences on the board.

ANSWER KEY
1. They discussed the sale of the house for hours and hours; finally,/then they agreed on a price.
2. Sabri Tahir was famous for his cleverness in business; therefore/consequently/as a result/for that reason, Durrell asked him for help in buying a house.
3. Durrell describes Sabri Tahir as having "an air of reptilian concentration and silence"; in other words/that is, Sabri was able to sit for a long time without moving or speaking but instead just watched.
4. There were people of different nationalities living in the village; mostly/for the most part/to some extent/to a large extent, they got along well without many problems.

C. Sentence Combining: More Adverbial Conjunctions

○ Go over the directions.
○ Read the first pair of sentences. Elicit adverbial conjunctions that could be used (*however*).
○ Have students combine the sentences and then compare sentences in pairs.
○ Call on students to read their sentences aloud.

ANSWER KEY
Answers may vary.
1. For many years, the country had a socialist economy; however, now it has a capitalist economy.
2. The taxes on their farm were very high, and they weren't getting good prices for their crops; as a result, they sold the farm and moved to the city.
3. She studied the language of the country that she was going to live in; in addition, she learned as much as possible about the culture.
4. The demand for that book is greater than the supply; in other words, there are more people who want to buy the book than there are copies of it.

EXPANSION ACTIVITY: First Sentences
○ Model the activity. Say a sentence about the information in the chapter (*The economic system of Korea is a command economy.*), and then give an adverbial conjunction (*however*). Elicit sentences from the class that complete the thought (*However, the economic system in China is mixed.*). Another example would be *The man had a lot of extra prairie dogs* with the adverbial conjunction *as a result*.
○ Have students write a first sentence about something related to the topics in the chapter and choose an appropriate adverbial conjunction.
○ Call on a student to read a sentence and adverbial conjunction and call on a classmate to finish the sentence.
○ Continue until everyone has had a chance to participate.

Recognizing and Repairing Run-Ons and Comma Splices
○ Go over the information in the box.
○ Ask comprehension questions: *What is a run-on sentence? What is a comma splice? What are ways we can repair a run-on sentence or comma splice?*

D. Recognizing and Repairing Run-On Sentences and Comma Splices
○ Go over the directions.
○ Have students identify the sentences as run-ons, comma splices, or okay, and then correct the run-ons and comma splices.
○ Have students check their answers in pairs.
○ Go over the answers with the class.

ANSWER KEY
Answers may vary.
1. R; These people are hunter-gatherers; in other words, they hunt animals for meat and gather fruits and vegetables.
2. R; The tribe hunts and gathers in one area; then they move on when there is no more food.
3. CS; Each person in the tribe has a job to do; for example, the young girls find water and firewood.
4. R; Men do most of the hunting, and women do most of the gathering.
5. OK
6. R; There is a lot of diversity in the diet; as a result, the people are generally healthy.
7. OK

E. Review: Finding Errors
○ Go over the directions. Remind students that finding errors is an important test-taking skill.
○ Have students circle the letter of the incorrect word or phrase in each sentence.
○ Have students compare answers in pairs.
○ Go over the answers with the class. Discuss how each error can be corrected.

ANSWER KEY
1. C; 2. C; 3. C; 4. C; 5. A

EXPANSION ACTIVITY: Editing Practice
❍ Photocopy and distribute the Black Line Master *Editing Practice* on page BLM 3.
❍ Go over the directions.
❍ Have students correct the mistakes and then compare answers with a partner.
❍ Go over the answers with the class.

ANSWER KEY

The San people of southern Africa represent a number of different tribes and languages. For the most part ⋀ they are hunter-gatherers. Sometimes the San work for farmers and ranchers. However, after a long drought, resources are scarce ⋀ the San return to hunting and gathering to make better use of the limited resources. In the past, conflict was sometimes create^d ⋀ when farmers took land or water that the San hunter-gatherers considered their own, or when livestock i̶s̶ ⋀^was stolen by the hunter-gatherers for food. Sometimes an agreement ⋀^was reached when the hunter-gatherers received food and protection in exchange for working as livestock herders or as hunters. Governments sometimes allowed farmers and traders to attack the San who resisted /⋀ ⋀^{As a consequence,} the number of hunter-gatherers was significantly reduced.

Edits shown in the answer key:
- "For the most part ⋀ they" → insert comma
- "resources are scarce ⋀ the San" → insert "; as a result,"
- "conflict was sometimes create^d"
- "when livestock i̶s̶ ⋀^was stolen"
- "an agreement ⋀^was reached"
- "San who resisted /⋀ ⋀^{As a consequence,} the number"

PART ⑤ ACADEMIC WRITING, PAGES 60–64

Writing Assignment
❍ Go over the writing assignment.
❍ Call on students to read the six steps aloud. Explain that they will always follow these steps for writing their paragraphs.

❍ Direct students' attention to Step A and have students choose the country they were born in, the country they live in now, or any other country whose economy they know something about.

WRITING STRATEGY: Writing a Topic Sentence
❍ Go over the information in the box.
❍ Ask comprehension questions: *Where do we usually put the topic sentence? What are the functions of a topic sentence? What is a controlling idea? What words are not good to use in the topic sentence? Why not?*

Writing a Topic Sentence
❍ Go over the directions.
❍ Have students work in small groups to choose the best topic sentence and say why the other sentences are not as good.
❍ Call on students to share their ideas with the class.

ANSWER KEY
1. C; A and B are too vague, and don't really express a controlling idea. A uses *fun*, a general adjective.
2. A; B is too large a topic for one paragraph and C is too general.
3. C; A and B are too general; A uses *interesting*, a general adjective.
4. B; A and C are too general, and C uses *difficult*, a general adjective.
5. B; A is too general and C is an example (too specific).

Improving Topic Sentences
❍ Go over the directions.
❍ Have students rewrite the sentences.
❍ Have students compare their sentences in small groups.
❍ Call on students to share their ideas with the class.

ANSWER KEY
Answers will vary.

○ Go over the directions for Step B.
○ Have students write a topic sentence.
○ Put students in pairs to read and provide feedback on topic sentences.

EXPANSION ACTIVITY: Suggestions for Improvement

○ Have students write their topic sentences on index cards or slips of paper.
○ Collect the topic sentences and choose several sentences to work on with the class.
○ Write several problematic sentences on the board. Discuss how to improve each one.
○ Have students rewrite the sentences.

WRITING STRATEGY: Writing a Paragraph of Analysis

○ Go over the information in the box.
○ Ask comprehension questions: *What do we do in a paragraph of analysis? What usually comes after the topic sentence? Where do we put specific details? What do we do in the last sentence of the paragraph?*
○ You may want to read the example paragraph aloud as students follow silently in their books.
○ Go over the points for students to notice in the example, and have them find each of the elements in the paragraph.
○ Read the *Analysis* directions. Ask students to highlight the five adverbial conjunctions and the associated punctuation in the example.
○ Go over answers with the class.

ANSWER KEY

Students should highlight the following:
    For the most part
    For example
    However
    In addition
    In short

TOEFL® iBT Tip

TOEFL iBT Tip 6: Both the integrated and independent essays of the TOEFL iBT are scored based on how well the examinee completes the overall writing task.

○ Point out that the *Writing a Paragraph of Analysis* strategy will help students to improve their coherence and link the flow of ideas in their independent essays by taking smaller steps in their essay development.

○ Remind students that working at the paragraph level and demonstrating the ability to support their opinions more concisely will likely improve their overall essay scores.

Independent writing tasks may require that examinees analyze an idea, present an opinion or perception about a topic, or develop an argument about a controversial issue.

Essay statements may be phrased in the following formats:
    Do you agree or disagree with the following statement?
    Some people believe X while other people believe Y. Which of these positions do you agree with?

○ Go over Step C and the three suggestions to plan their paragraphs. You may wish to model the steps for the students by writing a topic sentence on the board, listing support and specific examples.

CRITICAL THINKING STRATEGY: Analysis

Analysis is an important critical thinking strategy that students will use throughout the text, especially in the Part 5 Writing Strategy focus box. The analysis strategy involves breaking something down into parts and then examining the parts to determine their relationships to each other and to the whole. By using the graphic organizer in the next step, students can more easily see the parts and relationships in their paragraphs.

○ Photocopy and distribute the Black Line Master *Outlining a Paragraph of Analysis* on page BLM 4.

○ As students work on Step C, walk around the room and provide help as needed.

Writing Note

○ In Step C, students will need to decide on the order for their evidence. You may want to elicit ideas for various organizational schemes. For example, students might want to list evidence in increasing or decreasing order of importance. Often we put the strongest support last.

○ Direct students' attention to Step D. Have students write paragraphs, using the notes in Step C. Remind students that they will edit and revise in the next step.

○ Direct students' attention to Step E. Have students read and edit their paragraphs, using the questions as a guide. You may wish to have students circle or underline the elements in their paragraphs.

○ To encourage peer editing, have students exchange paragraphs with a partner, edit, and return to the writer. Remind students that peer editing will help them improve editing skills.

○ Direct students' attention to Step F. Go over the directions. Have students rewrite the paragraphs and hand them in to you.

○ After you have read and returned students' paragraphs, you may want to set aside time for students to read each other's writing or display the paragraphs in the classroom. Have students keep all of their final versions in a notebook or folder so that they can see their progress and improvement over time.

Unit 1 Vocabulary Workshop

Have students review vocabulary from Chapters 1 and 2.

A. Matching
❍ Go over the directions.
❍ Have students match words with definitions.

ANSWER KEY
1. f; 2. g; 3. a; 4. b; 5. c; 6. i; 7. d; 8. j; 9. h; 10. e

B. Words in Phrases: Prepositions
❍ Go over the directions.
❍ Have students write the prepositions on the line.

ANSWER KEY
1. of; 2. at; 3. of; 4. to; 5. on; 6. of; 7. between; 8. to

C. Vocabulary Expansion
❍ Go over the directions.
❍ Have students complete the chart.

ANSWER KEY

	Verb	Noun	Adjective
1.	determine	determination	determined
2.		nomad	nomadic
3.	distribute	distribution	distributed, distributive
4.	regulate	regulation	regulated, regular
5.	tend	tendency	

Stems and Affixes
❍ Go over the information in the box.
❍ Ask: *What is the difference between a prefix and a suffix? How many words can you think of that start with* multi–?

D. Stems and Affixes
❍ Go over the directions.
❍ Have students analyze the words in pairs.

ANSWER KEY
Answers may vary.
1. wrong idea; 2. between different countries;
3. focused on own ethnicity; 4. belief in Buddha;
5. of many countries

E. The Academic Word List
❍ Go over the directions.
❍ Have students write the correct words on the lines.

ANSWER KEY
1. economic; 2. intervene; 3. individual; 4. factors;
5. over; 6. items; 7. jobs; 8. labor; 9. globalization;
10. assumes; 11. purchase; 12. cultural; 13. require;
14. appropriate

UNIT 2 ●●●●● ART

❍ Direct students' attention to the photo on page 69. Ask questions: *Who do you see in the picture? Where do you think she lives? Why? What is she doing?*

❍ Write *art* on the board and help students brainstorm words related to art. Ask: *What topics do you think will be in this unit?* Circle the words they suggest.

CHAPTER 3 THEMES AND PURPOSES

In Part 1 of this chapter, students will read about how to look at art. In Part 2, they will read about religious art. In Part 3, students will learn about art and everyday life. Part 4 focuses on the mechanics of writing, including appositives, adjective clauses, participial phrases, prepositional phrases, order of adjectives, and transitional expressions of comparison and contrast. Finally, in Part 5, students will write a paragraph of comparison and contrast.

VOCABULARY

abolitionist	cloak	fierce	intermediary	point of view	tomb
afterlife	concrete	flourish	jade	portray	transform
analyze	depict	funeral	landscape	scribe	tree limb
ancestor	descendant	genre	livestock	shaman	visible
animated	describe	halo	manuscript	slavery	wagon
anthropomorphic	draw	hut	masterpiece	spiritual	
bare	faith	illuminate	meditation	stare	
cattle	fervent	infant	overseer	surround	

READING STRATEGIES

Determining Point of View
Guessing the Meaning from Context: Pictures and
  Captions
Finding Main Ideas: Major Sub-Topics
Understanding Italics

CRITICAL THINKING STRATEGIES

Thinking Ahead (Parts 1, 2, and 3)
**Comparing and Contrasting Two Works of Art
  (Part 2)**
Analysis (Part 5)
Making Connections (Part 3)
Note: The strategy in bold is highlighted in the
  student book.

MECHANICS

Appositives
Adjective Clauses
Participial Phrases
Prepositional Phrases
Adjectives
Order of Adjectives
Transitional Expressions: Comparison-Contrast

WRITING STRATEGIES

Gathering Supporting Material
Writing a Paragraph of Comparison-Contrast

TEST-TAKING STRATEGY

Understanding Pronouns

CHAPTER 3   Themes and Purposes

Chapter 3 Opener, page 71

❍ Direct students' attention to the chapter title and photo.
❍ Discuss the questions with the class.

PART ① INTRODUCTION
LOOKING AT ART: WHAT'S THE STORY?, PAGES 72–75

EXPANSION ACTIVITY: Sort by Category

❍ This activity is meant to warm students up to the topics and help them anticipate content. Explain the activity. Tell students that you will give them a question to ask classmates. They will then move around the classroom, asking the question and standing with people who have the same or similar answers to the question.

❍ Write on the board a variety of types of art (e.g., *painting, drawing, sculpture, photography*). Ask: *What's your favorite type of art?* Remind students to move around and talk to each other so that they can group themselves according to response. When students are grouped, ask each group what they represent.

❍ Have students return to their seats. Then ask additional questions related to the topics in the chapter. Create your own or use the ones below.
What period of art do you like best?
How good an artist are you?
If you could be good or better at some form of art, what would it be?
What is your favorite art museum?

Before Reading

A. Thinking Ahead

❍ Have students look at the photo and read the questions.
❍ Have students discuss the questions in pairs.
❍ Call on students to share their ideas with the class.

ANSWER KEY
Answers will vary.
1. hard to tell; looks more like a man
2. carrying a bowl
3. clay
4. formed by hand, maybe baked in an oven
5. fair condition; cracks visible
6. Answers will vary, but the correct answer is D.

B. Discussion

❍ Read the directions.
❍ Have students discuss the questions in small groups.
❍ Call on students to share their ideas with the class.

🎧 Reading

❍ Have students look at the reading.
❍ Go over the directions and the question.
❍ Have students read silently, or have students follow along silently as you play the audio program.

Culture Notes
❍ The Edomites are written about in both Jewish and Christian texts. There was hostility between the Edomites and the Israelites, with the Edomites refusing to let the Israelites pass through Edom in their escape from Egypt. Edom was located in what is now western Jordan, south of the Dead Sea.

○ King Josiah ruled Judah around 600 B.C.E. He outlawed the worship of pagan gods and tried to reunite Judah and Israel.

○ B.C. is the abbreviation for Before Christ and refers to the years before Christ. Time is accounted for backwards from the year of Christ's birth. A.D. is the abbreviation for *Anno Domini*, the year of Christ's birth. The abbreviations B.C.E. (Before Common Era) and C.E. (Common Era) are often used instead of B.C. and A.D. so as to be more neutral in terms of religious significance.

EXPANSION ACTIVITY: The Passive Voice

○ Briefly review the passive voice with students (Chapter 2, page 55).

○ Have students find and underline examples of the passive voice in *Looking at Art: What's the Story?*

○ Elicit examples from students and ask why the passive voice was used. *(Passive is used when it is not important or not known who the person or people are.)*

ANSWER KEY

Students should underline the following:
How are the various parts organized?
When, where, and by whom was it made?
How was the artist influenced by the world around him or her?
The figure is made of clay.
. . . the body of the figure is round, shaped almost like a cylinder . . .
. . . it was found in Israel . . .
Possibly, it was broken in the seventh century . . .

After Reading

READING STRATEGY: Determining Point of View

○ Go over the information in the box.

○ Ask comprehension questions: *What is point of view? How can we figure out a writer's point of view? Why is understanding point of view important?*

A. Determining Point of View

○ Go over the directions.

○ Have students discuss the question in pairs.

○ Go over the answers with the class.

ANSWER KEY

The author seems to prefer art history because it is history that makes the art come alive. In references to history, he says *important, mysterious,* and *alive.*

TOEFL® iBT Tip

TOEFL iBT Tip 1: The TOEFL iBT tests the ability to make inferences or draw conclusions based on what is implied in a passage. Examinees may be required to demonstrate an understanding of why an author explains concepts in a certain way.

○ Point out that the *Determining Point of View* activity requires students to draw conclusions and form generalizations based on information presented in the reading.

○ By understanding the author's point of view and opinion, students will be able to make assumptions and apply this skill to the reading section of the TOEFL iBT.

On the TOEFL iBT, this question may appear in the following format:
Why does the author state . . .?

CRITICAL THINKING STRATEGY: Applying Knowledge

Applying knowledge is an important critical thinking strategy. When we use what we learned in a reading to understand and interpret new information, we are applying knowledge.

B. Application

○ Direct students' attention to the three pictures. Point out that C is a photograph. Ask: *What time period is shown in each piece? Which picture do you prefer?*
○ Go over the directions.
○ Have students discuss the pictures in small groups, using the art criticism approach.
○ Have students fill in the chart on page 75.
○ Call on students to share their ideas with the class.

ANSWER KEY

Answers will vary.

Piece of art	List the components: people, things, and shapes.	What is your opinion of it?	What do you already know about this piece?
A	– Lots of people, both adults and children, cars, buildings, a man rolling a tire – Looks tropical – Lots of vertical lines, circles on cars and tires	Will vary	Will vary
B	– An artist with artist supplies in a museum looking at a painting on the wall – More horizontal than vertical lines, circles and ovals in the palette, the shapes of faces and collars	Will vary	Will vary
C	– Streets, people in dark clothing walking, fences – Both vertical and horizontal lines at angles	Will vary	Will vary

EXPANSION ACTIVITY: What's Your Point of View?

○ Brainstorm a list of adjectives and adverbs that could be used to express a point of view. Make sure students understand that some adjectives may be neutral or descriptive (*red, quiet*) while others may be more opinionated or subjective (*beautiful, relaxing, irritating*).
○ Say a sentence about one of the pictures (*This is an important piece of art because it shows a particular scene very effectively.*). Elicit ideas from the students about their opinion of the picture.
○ Once students understand how adjectives and adverbs can be used to express point of view, tell students to write a sentence about each picture using such adjectives and adverbs. Remind students that they shouldn't state their opinion directly in this activity.
○ Put students in pairs to exchange and determine points of view for the sentences.
○ Call on students to read sentences to the class and elicit the points of view. Help students identify which words provided clues to the point of view.

PART ② GENERAL INTEREST READING THE SACRED REALM OF ART, PAGES 76–82

Before Reading

A. Thinking Ahead

○ Go over the directions.
○ Put students in small groups to brainstorm a list of religions. Then have them discuss art that is important to each. If this is challenging for students, do the activity together as a class.
○ Call on students to share their ideas with the class.

EXPANSION ACTIVITY: Religious Art Research

○ Your students may be unfamiliar with the types of art in various religions. To help them understand this topic better, you can assign them a religion to research either in the library or on the Internet. If students do not have easy access to information, as an alternative, bring art books into the classroom for students to use.

○ Photocopy and distribute Black Line Master *Religious Art Research* on page BLM 5.

○ Put students in small groups, or have students sort themselves by which religion they are interested in researching. Assign each group a major religion.

○ To search on the Internet, have students enter the name of the religion and the word "art," or refer them to the websites below. Have students complete the worksheet *Religious Art Research*.

○ Return students to their small groups to compare charts.

○ Call on groups to report to the class on what they learned about that religion's art. If possible, have students show pictures of the art.

Useful websites:
• Islamic Arts and Architecture (IAAO)
  http://www.islamicart.com/
• Islamic Art at Los Angeles County Museum of Art
  http://www.lacma.org/islamic_art/islamic.htm
• Metropolitan Museum of Art
  http://www.metmuseum.org/Works_of_Art/department.asp?dep=14
• Buddha Dharma Education Association
  http://www.buddhanet.net/gallery.htm
• Buddhist Studies WWW Virtual Library
  http://kaladarshan.arts.ohio-state.edu/anu/buddhart.html
• Pacific Asia Museum
  http://www.pacificasiamuseum.org/buddhism/
• Office of Resources for International and Area Studies
  http://ias.berkeley.edu/orias/visuals/japan_visuals/shinto.HTM
• Kyoto National Museum
  http://www.kyohaku.go.jp/eng/tokubetsu/tokubetsu.html
• Hebrew Museum of Jerusalem
  http://www.hum.huji.ac.il/cja/
• Sherwin Miller Museum of Jewish Art
  http://www.jewishmuseum.net/
• Princeton University, Index of Christian Art
  http://ica.princeton.edu/
• Medieval and Early Christian Art
  http://www.usask.ca/antiquities/Collection/Medieval_Art.html
• San Antonia College, Early Hindu Art in India
  http://www.accd.edu/sac/vat/arthistory/arts1303/India2.htm
• University of Michigan, Hindu Art
  http://www.umich.edu/~hartspc/acsaa/Acsaa/indexlist/hindu.html

B. Vocabulary Preparation

○ Go over the directions.

○ Read the first sentence aloud. Elicit the part of speech for *visible* and possible meanings.

○ Have students write the part of speech and then a guess about the meaning of each word.

○ Have students compare their answers in pairs.

○ Go over the answers with the class.

ANSWER KEY

1. adjective, can be seen; 2. adjective, related to spirit/God/religion; 3. verb, grew/survived/thrived; 4. verb, shows; 5. adjective (a noun modifier), baby; 6. verb, showed

EXPANSION ACTIVITY: Short Short Stories

○ Have students write paragraphs in which they use all of the new words in Activity B, *Vocabulary Preparation*. Tell students that the sentences must make sense, and that they should try to fit all of the words in as few sentences as possible.

○ Set a time limit of five minutes. You may want to have students work in pairs.

○ Call on students to read their paragraphs to the class.

READING STRATEGY: Guessing the Meaning from Context: Pictures and Captions

❍ Go over the information in the box.
❍ Ask: *What are captions? How can pictures or captions help you understand new words?*

C. Pictures and Captions

❍ Go over the directions.
❍ Have students write the words on the lines.
❍ Go over the answers with the class.

TOEFL® iBT Tip

TOEFL iBT Tip 2: The TOEFL iBT measures the ability to understand specific words and phrases selected by the author and used in the passage.

❍ Point out that the strategy and activity for *Guessing the Meaning from Context: Pictures and Captions* will help students improve their vocabulary for the TOEFL iBT. Often, a passage may be accompanied by an image, drawing, or table to help the examinee better understand the passage. This is a helpful tool for overall basic comprehension in both academic and nonacademic settings.

READING STRATEGY: Finding Main Ideas: Major Sub-Topics

❍ Go over the information in the box.
❍ Ask questions: *What two things does an introduction often include? What order are the sub-topics listed in?*

∩ Reading

❍ Go over the directions and the questions. Have students highlight the answers as they read.
❍ Have students read *The Sacred Realm of Art* silently, or have them follow along silently as you play the audio program.

ANSWER KEY

Art makes something spiritual visible. It also portrays important people and events in the religion.
Subtopics: The ancient Olmecs, the Bwa, Buddhism, Christianity

After Reading

A. Check Your Understanding

❍ Go over the directions.
❍ Have students review the reading and the sentences they highlighted to answer the questions and complete the chart.
❍ Have students compare answers with a partner.
❍ Go over the answers with the class.

ANSWER KEY

1. Art attempts to take something invisible, something spiritual, and make it visible.

2.

Religion	One Example of a Piece of Art from This Religion
ancient Olmec	Olmec figure, maybe a shaman, holding an infant man-jaguar
Bwa	Masks that show nature spirits, called on when the help of spirits is needed
Buddhism	Tathagata Buddha
Christianity	The Virgin Mary holding the infant Jesus surrounded by angels

B. Vocabulary Check

❍ Go over the directions.
❍ Have students write the words on the lines.
❍ Go over the answers with the class.

ANSWER KEY

1. faith; 2. concrete; 3. shaman, intermediary; 4. funerals;
5. ancestors

C. Vocabulary Expansion

○ Go over the directions.
○ Have students use dictionaries to complete the chart and then compare answers with a partner.
○ Go over the answers with the class.

ANSWER KEY

Buddhism, Buddhist, Buddhist
Hinduism, Hindu, Hindu
Judaism, Jewish, Jew
Christianity, Christian, Christian
Islam, Islamic/Muslim, Muslim

TEST-TAKING STRATEGY: Understanding Pronouns

○ Go over the information in the box.
○ Ask: *Why do writers use pronouns?*

D. Understanding Pronouns

○ Go over the directions.
○ Have students highlight the noun or noun phrase the pronoun refers to.
○ Call on students to share their answers with the class.

ANSWER KEY

These words should be highlighted:
1. *something spiritual;* 2. *The creature;* 3. *Masks;*
4. *the Buddha;* 5. *The bodhisattvas*

TOEFL® iBT Tip

TOEFL iBT Tip 3: The TOEFL iBT measures the ability to identify the relationships between pronouns and their antecedents (words that precede them) or postcedents (words that follow them) in a passage.

○ Point out that the strategy and activity for *Understanding Pronouns* will help students improve their ability to correctly identify and link pronouns and nouns on the TOEFL iBT.

On the TOEFL iBT, this question may appear in the following format:
   *The word **it** in the passage refers to . . .*

CRITICAL THINKING STRATEGY: Comparing and Contrasting Two Works of Art

○ Go over the information in the box.
○ Ask: *What is one way to compare two things? What is a graphic organizer that can help you contrast two things?*

E. Comparing and Contrasting Two Works of Art

○ Go over the directions. Explain to students that the Tathagata Buddha is not the title of the piece; it is merely what it is called. The artist is unknown and no title was given to the art. This is why Tathagata Buddha is not in italics, unlike the titles of other pieces of art in the chapter.
○ Have students list similarities and then write differences on the T-chart.
○ Put students in pairs to compare their ideas.
○ Call on students to share their ideas with the class.

ANSWER KEY

Similarities:

Central figures are sitting and facing front.

Central figures are the largest.

They are surrounded by figures with halos. These figures are helping others reach their goals (heaven, Nirvana).

Differences:

A Tathagata Buddha	*Madonna Enthroned*
In meditation	Sitting on throne
Hands in mudra	Gesturing to Jesus
Surrounded by bodhisattvas	Holding a baby
	Surrounded by angels

TOEFL® iBT Tip

TOEFL iBT Tip 4: The TOEFL iBT tests the ability to understand facts, examples, and explanations in a text; however, it does not directly test understanding of the main idea of a passage. Examinees may also need to understand a compare-contrast text and be able to classify that information into different components.

○ The activity *Comparing and Contrasting Two Works of Art* demonstrates how using a graphic organizer enables students to visually connect information. This will help to scaffold students' abilities upward toward mastering the schematic table questions on the test.

F. Discussion

○ Go over the directions.

○ Have students discuss the questions in small groups.

○ Call on students to share their ideas with the class.

ANSWER KEY

Answers will vary.

PART ③ ACADEMIC READING
ART AS THE MIRROR OF EVERYDAY LIFE, PAGES 83–91

Before Reading

A. Thinking Ahead

○ Go over the directions.

○ Have students discuss the pictures on pages 85 and 86.

○ Call on students to share their ideas with the class.

○ Direct students' attention to the title of the reading that starts on page 85. Talk about what the title might mean.

ANSWER KEY

Answers will vary.

B. Vocabulary Preparation

○ Go over the directions.

○ Have students match the definition to the words and then check their answers with a partner.

○ Go over the answers with the class.

ANSWER KEY

1. b; 2. c; 3. a; 4. f; 5. e; 6. g; 7. d

C. Vocabulary in Pictures and Captions

○ Go over the directions.

○ Have students write their guesses on the lines and then compare answers with a partner.

○ You may want to have students look the words up in a dictionary to confirm their guesses before going over their answers.

○ Go over the answers with the class.

ANSWER KEY

Answers will vary.
1. a house or building; 2. scenery, surrounding land;
3. coat; 4. cows; 5. cart, something pulled by horses
that you ride in; 6. tree branch without leaves; 7. looks

EXPANSION ACTIVITY: Beanbag Toss

❍ Give students one minute to review the new words in Activities B and C.
❍ Call on a student and toss a ball or beanbag to the student as you say one of the new words. Elicit its meaning from the student.
❍ Tell the student to call on a classmate, toss the ball or beanbag, and say a new word.
❍ Continue until everyone has had a chance to participate. As a variation, students can say the definition and elicit the new word.

Reading

❍ Go over the directions before the reading. Read the question aloud.
❍ Have students read the article silently, or play the audio program and have students follow along silently.
❍ Elicit ideas from the students for the story behind each piece of art.

Grammar Notes

❍ You may want to point out that in this reading, the author sometimes lists items separated by commas but without a final *and* (for example, *the teacher, the house, the dog* and *to record, to please the eye, to make us smile*). This is a stylistic variation, not how lists are typically written.
❍ Students may notice that the writer uses the first person plural in this passage (*we, our*). Most academic readings do not use this point of view. In this case, it is used to show that we are the audience, standing back and looking at the art together.

Pronunciation Notes

❍ You may want to remind students about the intonation pattern when we list items—we use rising intonation on each item until the last when we use falling intonation.
❍ Read and have students repeat sentences with lists in lines 2, 8, and 9 in the reading. For example:

mother and father, sisters and brothers, the teacher,

the house, the dog.

After Reading

A. Making Connections

❍ Go over the directions.
❍ Have students choose a piece of art and then complete the chart.
❍ Put students in small groups to discuss their charts. You may want to put students first into small groups according to the piece of art they chose, and then reconfigure the groups so that one student in each group represents each of the four pieces.
❍ Call on students to share their ideas with the class.

ANSWER KEY

Here are possible answers for each of the pieces of art

Title of the piece	Art Criticism • Describe it. What people and things are there? • What are the details and space relationships?	Art History • When, where, and by whom was it made? • How was the artist influenced by the world around him or her? • How important is the work?
Court Ladies Preparing Newly Woven Silk	Three women and a girl stretch and iron a piece of silk. A little girl peeks underneath. Background is empty. Atmosphere of pleasant shared work Gentle and quiet	12th century China Scene of daily activity
"February" page *Les Tres Riches Heures du Duc de Berry*	Hut with three people around a fire Clothes pulled back for warmth Snow-covered landscape Sheep and birds and three men One man rushing toward the hut with cloak over his face Man chopping wood Man walking up hill with donkey Church in background Calendar at top Cold, busy	Middle ages (early 15th century) Illuminated page of book Each page shows a seasonal activity. Wealthy people paid artists to hand-paint books.
Model of counting of livestock from tomb of Meketre	Meketre seated on chair in the shade, in center of model Son on left, scribes on right Overseers stand nearby. Men herd cattle in front of Meketre so scribes can count them. Herders' gestures are animated. Cattle have beautiful markings. Scene is busy, prosperous.	Model from tomb of Meketre, Deir el-Bahri, Dynasty 11, 2134-1991 B.C.E. Painted wood Model was made to make sure that Meketre, an Egyptian official, had a good afterlife.
John Brown Going to His Hanging	John Brown at center against white jailhouse in background Brown's arms are bound. People on wagon dressed in black Wagon drawn by two white horses, symbolizing black-white drama Bare tree limb, symbolizing hanging tree, death A black woman at far right turns her back on the scene and stares out fiercely, arms crossed in anger. Artist may be criticizing the event.	Painted in 1942 by Horace Pippin Based on event from 1850s John Brown was an abolitionist, trying to free slaves. Brown was found guilty and hanged on December 2, 1859. Pippin's grandmother witnessed the event. Black-white drama of historical event

B. Vocabulary Check
○ Go over the directions.
○ Have students write the correct words on the lines and then check their answers with a partner.
○ Go over the answers with the class.

ANSWER KEY
1. genre; 2. illuminate; 3. afterlife; 4. scribes;
5. abolitionists; 6. descendant; 7. transformed; 8. drawn

EXPANSION ACTIVITY: Word-Pictures
○ Explain that in this activity, students will draw an image based on a "word-picture," like the painter Horace Pippin did with his grandmother's "word-picture." Students will work in pairs. One student will describe an event that he or she witnessed or took part in while the other student turns the word-picture into a drawing. Then they will switch roles.
○ Put students in pairs to take turns creating word-pictures and drawings.
○ Call on students to show their drawings and tell the class about their partner's event.

READING STRATEGY: Understanding Italics
○ Go over the information in the box.
○ Ask: *What are italics? Why do we use them?*

Academic Notes
○ When writing for academic purposes, it is very important to use the correct style for the titles of books, magazine articles, works of art, and so on. While most titles are written in italics, titles of short works such as poems, essays, and short stories, are often placed within quotation marks. Students should always check with instructors to see what format style should be followed. Some instructors may prefer that students underline titles rather than italicize them.
○ When writing by hand, students should use underlining rather than italics.

○ Some students tend to overuse italics for emphasis. Remind students that italics for emphasis must be used only on occasion.

C. Understanding Italics
○ Go over the directions.
○ Have students find the words in italics and give a reason for the italics.
○ Go over the answers with the class.

ANSWER KEY
Mudra: foreign word
Bodhisattvas: foreign word
Living with Art: Title
Court Ladies Preparing Newly Woven Silk: Title
Les Tres Riches Heures: Title
February: Title
John Brown Going to His Hanging: Title

D. Vocabulary Expansion: A Game
○ Go over the directions.
○ Put students in small groups to complete the chart.
○ Call on students to share their ideas with the class.

ANSWER KEY
Possible answers

Opinion	Size	Condition or Quality
finest	grand	quiet
charming	small	gentle
delightful		famous
pleasant		seasonal
beautiful		snow-covered
		earthly
		professional
		personal
		fervent
		violent
		guilty
		bare
		symbolic
		lone
		simple
		daily
		wealthy

ANSWER KEY, continued

Age	Color	Nationality
early/earliest	pastel white black	Chinese French Egyptian

E. Word Journal
○ Go over the directions.
○ Have students write words in their Word Journals.

F. Application
○ Go over the directions. For a variation, see the following expansion activity.
○ Put students in small groups to share their ideas.
○ Call on students to share their ideas with the class.

EXPANSION ACTIVITY: Compare Paintings
○ Photocopy and distribute the Black Line Master *Comparing Paintings* on page BLM 6.
○ Have students complete the Venn diagram to compare and contrast two of the paintings.
○ Have students use the Venn diagram to write several sentences about how the paintings are similar and/or different.

G. Response Writing
○ Go over the directions.
○ Explain that this is a quick-writing activity and does not have to be perfect. Point out that response writing can be a warm-up to a more structured writing assignment, helping to generate ideas.
○ Set a time limit of 10 minutes.
○ Put students in pairs to read or talk about their writing.

🖥 Website Research
○ For additional information on art history and art criticism, refer students to these websites:
  • Art History, Dr. Christopher Witcombe
    http://witcombe.sbc.edu/ARTHLinks.html
  • Art History Network
    http://www.arthistory.net/
  • Metropolitan Museum of Art, Timeline of Art History
    http://www.metmuseum.org/toah/splash.htm

• Art History Research Centre
  http://www.harmsen.net/ahrc/
• University of Michigan
  http://art-design.umich.edu/mother/
• Journal of Aesthetics and Art Criticism
  http://www.jstor.org/journals/00218529.html

PART ④ THE MECHANICS OF WRITING, PAGES 92–99

Read through the introduction to Part 4 with students.

TOEFL® iBT Tip

TOEFL iBT Tip 5: Although the TOEFL iBT does not discretely test grammar skills, examinees' essay scores will be determined based on the range of grammatical accuracy and sophistication of vocabulary used in their essays.

○ Point out that the grammar activities in *The Mechanics of Writing* part of this chapter will help them improve their abilities to write compare-contrast essays by using appositives, adjectives, prepositional phrases, and transitions. It will also help students learn to edit their essays for subject-verb agreement and word order.

Appositives
○ Go over the information in the box about appositives.
○ Ask comprehension questions: *What is an appositive? Where do we put appositives? What kind of punctuation do we use with appositives?*

A. Sentence Combining: Appositives
○ Go over the directions.
○ Have students combine the sentences, making the second sentence an appositive.
○ Go over the answers with the class.

ANSWER KEY
1. This is from the tomb of Meketre, an Egyptian official.
2. A 13th-century Italian master, Cimabue, painted *Madonna Enthroned.*
3. The Buddha's hand position, a *mudra,* symbolizes the giving of gifts.
4. Mary Cassatt, a famous American painter, lived in France.
5. Cartier-Bresson, a well-known French photographer, took this photo at what he called the "decisive moment."

EXPANSION ACTIVITY:
Describe Your Partner
○ Explain the activity. Students will take turns interviewing a partner and then writing sentences with appositives.
○ Put students in pairs to interview each other for two minutes.
○ Have students write sentences with appositives about their partners.
○ Call on students to share their sentences with the class.

Adjective Clauses
○ Go over the information in the box.
○ Ask: *What does an adjective clause do? Where does it go?*

Grammar Note
○ Make sure that students understand that commas are only used when the information is extra and is not necessary for identification.

B. Sentence Combining: Adjective Clauses
○ Go over the directions.
○ Read the first pair of sentences. Elicit ways to combine the sentences.
○ Have students combine the sentences using the second sentence as an adjective clause.
○ Have students compare sentences in pairs.
○ Call on students to read their sentences to the class.

ANSWER KEY
1. He took a class in art history, which is a required course.
2. This figure is actually a perfume bottle, which looks like a doll.
3. The painting is a memorial to John Brown, who was a famous abolitionist.
4. Impressionist artists, whose work was not appreciated at the time it was created, are now favorites among museum goers.
5. The Buddha is surrounded by *bodhisattvas,* who help other people reach Nirvana.

Participial Phrases
○ Go over the information in the box.
○ Ask questions: *What is a participial phrase? How is it like an appositive? What are the two types of participial phrases?*

C. Participial Phrases
○ Go over the directions and the example.
○ Have students highlight each adjective clause and draw an arrow to the noun it modifies. Then have students change the clause to a participial phrase.
○ Have students compare their answers in pairs.
○ Go over the answers with the class. You may want to have students write the new sentences on the board.

ANSWER KEY
1. The central figure is surrounded by smaller figures ~~who are~~ wearing halos.
2. Two artists ~~who were~~ unknown to each other created similar works of art.
3. The anthropomorphic figure ~~that is~~ holding a small bowl is an incense burner.
4. The central figure, ~~who is~~ surrounded by angels, is the Virgin Mary.
5. The women ~~who are~~ folding the silk are court ladies.

ANSWER KEY, CONTINUED

6. The people ~~who are~~ working in the fields are peasants from the nearby village.

7. *Cooling Off by the River Bank,* ~~which was~~ painted many years before *In the Omnibus,* probably influenced Mary Cassatt.

8. Impressionist artists, ~~who were~~ unappreciated in their lifetime, are favorites among museum goers today.

Prepositional Phrases

○ Go over the information in the box.
○ Ask comprehension questions: *What is a prepositional phrase? What phrases might be useful in discussing a painting?*
○ Have students dictate to you additional sentences with prepositional phrases to describe the painting.

D. Prepositional Phrases

○ Go over the directions.
○ Have students use prepositional phrases to answer the questions about *February.*
○ Call on students to read sentences to the class.

ANSWER KEY

1. The calendar is at the top of the painting.
2. A single tree is in the middle of the picture (*or* in the background).
3. The three women are in the hut in the lower left-hand corner of the picture.
4. Some birds are in the foreground at the bottom of the picture.
5. The man with the donkey is in the background.
6. The forest is in the upper right-hand corner.

Adjectives

○ Go over the information in the box.
○ Ask comprehension questions: *What does an adjective do? Where do we put adjectives? How are participles used as adjectives?*

E. Brainstorming Adjectives

○ Go over the directions.
○ Have students look at the pictures and list as many adjectives as they can in each category.
○ Put students in pairs to compare ideas.
○ Elicit ideas from the class. Discuss adjectives that did not seem to fit any category.

ANSWER KEY

Answers will vary.

Order of Adjectives

○ Go over the information in the box.
○ Ask questions: *How would you describe a painting that is large and exciting? How would you describe a painting that is large and exciting and Canadian?*

Grammar Notes

○ Because students will have brainstormed adjectives in other categories, point out the order of other types of adjectives: opinion – size – age – shape – color – origin/nationality – material – purpose. Point out that although this is the usual order of adjectives, there may be exceptions.
○ Long strings of adjectives should be avoided. Usually two or three adjectives are sufficient.
○ Rules vary somewhat for the use of commas in a series of adjectives.

F. Order of Adjectives

○ Go over the directions and the example.
○ Have students add the adjectives to the sentences.
○ Have students check their answers with a partner.
○ Go over the answers with the class.

ANSWER KEY

1. It's a huge Italian statue.
2. There is a large unpainted house in the foreground.
3. This is a strange modern American painting.
4. These are uncomfortable small dark rooms.
5. It's a pleasant little Chinese scene.
6. In the foreground, there is a tired old black dog.

Transitional Expressions: Comparison-Contrast

○ Go over the information in the box.
○ Ask comprehension questions: *What transitional expressions tell us how things are similar? What transitional expressions can we use to talk about how things are different? Which expressions are adverbial conjunctions?*

G. Sentence Combining: Expressions of Comparison-Contrast

○ Go over the directions.
○ Read the first pair of sentences and elicit what transitional expression should be used and why.
○ Have students combine the sentences.
○ Have students check their answers with a partner.
○ Go over the answers with the class.

ANSWER KEY

Answers may vary.
1. The central figure of the Buddha isn't holding anything; in contrast, the Virgin Mary is holding the baby Jesus.
2. Both the Tathagata Buddha and *Madonna Enthroned* are religious paintings.
3. The Tathagata Buddha was created for Buddhists in Tibet, while *Madonna Enthroned* was created for Christian Italians.
4. Both the Buddha and the Virgin Mary have serene expressions.

H. Review: Finding Errors

○ Go over the directions.
○ Direct students' attention to the first item and elicit the letter of the section that contains the error (A). Elicit the error (There should be commas before and after *a Buddhist painting*).
○ Have students circle the letters of the errors and then compare answers with a partner.
○ Go over the answers with the class. Have students explain what the errors are and how to correct them. Students can write the corrected sentences on the board.

ANSWER KEY

1. A; 2. B; 3. A; 4. C; 5. B

EXPANSION ACTIVITY: Editing Practice

○ Photocopy and distribute the Black Line Master *Editing Practice* on page BLM 7.
○ Go over the directions.
○ Have students correct the mistakes and then compare answers with a partner.
○ Go over the answers with the class.

ANSWER KEY

Both *John Brown Going to His Hanging* and the model depicting the counting of livestock from the tomb of Meketre present scenes from everyday life, but they have many more differences than similarities. In the two pieces of art, there are crowds of people and at least one building. In the model, only an Egyptian (small) building is ^in the center. There are many men watching and count ^ing livestock. ^However ~~Similarly~~, in the painting of John Brown's hanging, there are several wooden buildings extend ^ing out to the side. ~~Like~~ ^Unlike the model, the people in the painting are facing away from the viewer. The background is very full in the painting/ ^ ^while In the model, you can't see trees or other buildings. In the painting, John Brown ^, the man in the center ^, is about to be killed, creat ^ing a moment of drama and excitement. In contrast ^, we can see a very ordinary activity in the model.

PART 5 ACADEMIC WRITING, PAGES 100–104

Writing Assignment
- Go over the description of the writing assignment in the box.
- Have students read the seven steps. Point out that there is an added step in this paragraph writing process: *grouping your supporting material.*
- Direct students' attention to Step A and have students choose one pair of paintings to write about. Encourage students to choose a pair of paintings that they can both compare and contrast as that will make for a better essay.
- Direct students' attention to Step B. Have students check which topic sentence in each pair they think is stronger. Elicit their answers and reasons. They should notice that sentence B in both pairs is very simple and will not lead to a rich written discussion.

WRITING STRATEGY: Gathering Supporting Material
- Go over the information in the box.
- Ask: *What is one way you can gather supporting information?*

Gathering Supporting Material
- Direct students' attention to Step C. Have students complete the chart with words and phrases to describe the two paintings they have chosen. You may want to put students in pairs to share their ideas.

CRITICAL THINKING STRATEGY: Analysis
Analysis is an important critical thinking strategy that incorporates comparing and contrasting. Remind students that the Venn diagram in Step D is an excellent way to compare and contrast in preparation for writing.

- Direct students' attention to Step D. Remind students the overlapping section shows similarities, and the other areas show differences.

- Have students complete the Venn diagram with the information from their charts. Walk around to monitor the process and provide help as needed.

WRITING STRATEGY: Writing a Paragraph of Comparison-Contrast
- Go over the information in the box.
- Ask comprehension questions: *What do we do when we compare? What do we do when we contrast two things? When you choose two things to compare and contrast, what do you need to pay attention to? What is one way to organize your paragraph? What should come last in your comparison-contrast paragraph?*
- You may want to read the example paragraph aloud as students follow silently in their books.
- Go over the points for students to notice in the example, and have them find each of the elements in the paragraph.
- Read the *Analysis* directions. Ask students to highlight the topic sentence, the conclusion, and transition expressions of comparison and contrast. Have students answer the questions.
- Go over answers with the class.

ANSWER KEY
Two religious paintings, the Tathagata Buddha from Tibet and Cimabue's *Madonna Enthroned* from Italy, were created four thousand miles apart and for different religions, so they are quite different in content; nevertheless, they are surprisingly similar in form. The Tathagata Buddha is, of course, a Buddhist painting, and *Madonna Enthroned* is Christian. The Buddha, the central figure in the Tathagata Buddha, isn't holding anything; in contrast, the Virgin Mary, the central figure in *Madonna Enthroned,* is holding the baby Jesus. The Buddha is wearing very little clothing except for elaborate jewelry, while the Virgin is wearing long robes. However, these paintings have more similarities than differences. Both were created in the 13th century and have a large central figure facing front. The central figure in each painting has a calm, serene expression and a symbolic hand gesture; the Buddha's hand position symbolizes the giving of gifts, while Mary gestures toward her son, symbolic of the hope of the world. Finally, both the Buddha and the Virgin Mary are surrounded by smaller figures wearing halos. In the Tathagata Buddha, these smaller figures, *bodhisattvas,* help people to reach Nirvana. Similarly, the angels

ANSWER KEY, continued

surrounding the Virgin Mary help people to reach heaven. <u>Clearly, two artists unknown to each other created quite similar paintings for their different religions.</u> Differences come first and similarities second because the writer wants to point out that the paintings are more similar than different.

TOEFL® iBT Tip

TOEFL iBT Tip 6: Both the integrated and independent essays of the TOEFL iBT are scored based on how well the examinee completes the overall writing task. Examinees may be required to compare and contrast points of view in a lecture and draw information from each source to show that contrast.

○ Point out that the strategy for *Writing a Paragraph of Comparison-Contrast* in this chapter will help students improve their coherence and link the flow of ideas in their essays by focusing on the paragraph level. The "process writing" approach will help students organize their thoughts and take meaningful steps toward developing their essays.

○ Remind students that working slowly, sentence-by-sentence, will help them develop their paragraphs more concisely, improve the organization of the essay, and likely improve their overall essay scores.

○ Direct students' attention to Step E. Have students write paragraphs, using the notes in Step D. Remind students that the title of a work of art should be underlined or in italics.

○ Direct students' attention to Step F. Go over the questions. Have students read and edit their paragraphs using the questions as a guide.

○ For peer editing, have students exchange paragraphs with a partner, edit, and return to the writer.

○ Go over the directions for Step G. Have students carefully rewrite their paragraphs and hand them in to you.

○ After you have read and returned students' paragraphs, you may want to set aside time for students to read each other's writing or display the paragraphs in the classroom. Have students keep all of their final versions in a notebook or folder so that they can see their progress and improvement over time.

EXPANSION ACTIVITY: Presentations

○ Bring in art books with large color illustrations. Students can work individually, in pairs, or in small groups. Students will choose two pieces of art to compare and contrast. Have students complete a Venn diagram about the two pieces.

○ Discuss with students what should be included in a visual presentation in contrast to a written paper. Stress the importance of having interesting visuals in the presentation, and the importance of looking at the audience while speaking (rather than reading notes or a paper).

○ Have students practice giving their presentations to each other, using only their Venn diagrams as notes. Remind them to give the names of the pieces of art, the artists, and the dates in the introduction. Give students a two-minute time limit to keep the presentations short and manageable.

○ Ask for volunteers to give their presentations to the class.

UNIT 2 ●●●●●● ART

CHAPTER 4 THE ANCIENT WORLD: EGYPT

In Part 1 of this chapter, students will read about the rules that govern Egyptian art. In Part 2, they will read a newspaper article about the findings of an archaeological dig and what the findings can tell us about life in ancient Egypt. In Part 3, students will read a brief history of Egyptian civilization. Part 4 focuses on the mechanics of writing, including infinitives of purpose, transitional expressions of cause and effect, and conjunctions and subordinating conjunctions. Finally, in Part 5, students will write a paragraph of cause and effect about a piece of Egyptian art.

VOCABULARY

aimlessly	dump	in vogue	playing around	skilled worker
artisan	dynasty	journey	pose	slope
blue-collar worker	excavation	keep up with the Joneses	profile	stability
cemetery	falcon	magnificent	put up with	succession
chariot	find	massive	recur	take a toll
cliff	found	monogamous	remain	torso
commoner	frozen	neatly trimmed	restore	treasure
continuity	go to great lengths	pharaoh	ruler	vizier
decree				

READING STRATEGIES
Guessing the Meaning from Context: Using Opposites
Recognizing Style: Newspaper Feature Stories
Guessing the Meaning from Context: *in other words, that is, i.e.*
Finding Evidence

CRITICAL THINKING STRATEGIES
Thinking Ahead (Parts 1, 2, and 3)
Applying Information (Part 1)
Identifying Causes and Effects (Part 2)
Analysis (Part 5)
Note: The strategy in bold is highlighted in the student book.

MECHANICS
Infinitives of Purpose
Transitional Expressions of Cause and Effect: Subordinating Conjunctions
Transitional Expressions and Phrases
Conjunctions of Cause and Effect: Review

WRITING STRATEGY
Writing a Paragraph of Cause and Effect

TEST-TAKING STRATEGIES
Understanding Idioms
Applying Information

CHAPTER 4   The Ancient World: Egypt

Chapter 4 Opener, page 105

○ Direct students' attention to the chapter title and photo on page 105. Read the questions aloud.
○ Put students in pairs or small groups to discuss the questions.
○ Call on students to share their ideas with the class.

Culture Note

○ The Great Sphinx of Giza, believed to have been built 4,500 years ago, is a massive statue with the head of a human and the body of a lion. Sphinx, which means "strangler," was a term used by the Greeks to describe a mythological creature. Egyptologists believe that the Great Sphinx was built during the rein of Khafre, a prosperous pharaoh who also built the great pyramids in the surrounding area.

PART ① INTRODUCTION
THE RULES OF EGYPTIAN ART, PAGES 106–109

Before Reading

EXPANSION ACTIVITY: Lineup

○ Explain the activity. Tell students that you will ask a series of questions. In answer to each question, students should line up to form a continuum with *a lot* on one side of the room, and *none at all* on the other. In order for students to place themselves in line, they will need to ask each other questions.

○ Have students stand. Ask: *How much do you know about art in general?* Indicate one side of the room for *a lot*, or *expert knowledge*, and the other for *no knowledge at all.* When students have formed their continuum, call on a couple of students to explain their position in the line.
○ Ask several more questions and have students move. Create your own or use the ones below. *How much do you know about Egyptian art? How much do you know about ancient history? How much do you know about other human wonders of the world?*
○ Point out that students who know a lot about Egypt and Egyptian art can help their classmates in this chapter. Keep this information in mind when grouping students.

Thinking Ahead

○ Have students look at the picture on page 106.
○ Go over the directions and questions.
○ Have students discuss the questions in small groups.
○ Call on students to share their ideas with the class.

ANSWER KEY

Answers may vary.
1. Nakht and his wife are the large figures on the left. Important people are often the largest.
2. servants
3. fighting, hunting, harvesting, bringing food and gifts
4. The figures are stiff, stylized, and always seen from the side.

🎧 Reading

○ Have students look at the reading.
○ Go over the directions and the question.
○ Have students read silently, or have students follow along silently as you play the audio program.

Culture Notes

◯ Plato was a Greek philosopher and writer who lived from 427 to 347 B.C.E. He studied under Socrates, and is best known for his *Republic.*

◯ Horus refers to a number of Egyptian gods, the most famous of whom was the son of Isis and Osiris. Horus usually is associated with kingship, the sky, and victory, and is often depicted as a hawk or a hawk-man.

◯ Narmer is thought to have lived around 3150 B.C.E., and was the first king of the first dynasty. The palette is supposed to commemorate the victory of Narmer's southern kingdom over the north.

◯ Nefertiti was the queen when Akhenaten was pharaoh of Egypt during the 14th century B.C.E.

After Reading

A. Check Your Understanding

◯ Go over the directions.
◯ Have students highlight the sentences in the reading that answer the questions.
◯ Go over the answers with the class.

ANSWER KEY

Line 43: *It wasn't due to a lack of ability. Egyptian artists were certainly able to create full, natural images.*
Line 50: *Nevertheless, the flat artistic style remained the same in most Egyptian art because the artists were following a strict set of rules written by powerful priests.*

B. Vocabulary Check

◯ Go over the directions.
◯ Have students match the definitions to the words by writing the letters on the lines.
◯ Have students check their answers in pairs.
◯ Go over the answers with the class.

ANSWER KEY

1. a; 2. g; 3. b; 4. j; 5. i; 6. c; 7. d; 8. f; 9. h; 10. e

C. Application

◯ Go over the directions.
◯ Have students complete the chart in pairs.
◯ Call on students to share their ideas with the class.

ANSWER KEY

Elements	Examples in the Wall Painting from the Tomb of Nakht	Rule
Space	The painting is full of figures, things, and writing. There is no empty space.	6
Animals	There are some birds in the top right, but they are not clearly visible.	5
People:		
color	Nakht is darker than his wife.	2
size	Nakht and wife are the largest figures.	1
actions	Nakht and his wife are frozen and unmoving. Other people are moving.	3, 4
style	Head, arms, and feet are in profile; shoulders and one eye are seen from front.	7

TOEFL® iBT Tip

TOEFL iBT Tip 1: The TOEFL iBT tests the ability to understand facts, examples, and explanations in a text; however, it does not directly test understanding of the main idea of a passage.

◯ Activity C, *Application*, requires students to visually connect information by searching for details in the text and filling in the chart. Remind students that being able to skim and scan to locate information is a technique that will help them with schematic table questions on the test.

PART ② GENERAL INTEREST READING

FINDS REVEAL MUCH OF LIFE AT PYRAMIDS, PAGES 110–116

Before Reading

A. Making Predictions
○ Go over the directions and the questions.
○ Have students work in pairs to discuss the questions.
○ Call on students to share their ideas with the class.

ANSWER KEY
Answers will vary.

B. Vocabulary Preparation
○ Go over the directions.
○ Read the first sentence aloud. Elicit possible definitions.
○ Have students work in pairs to write definitions.
○ Go over the answers with the class.

ANSWER KEY
Answers may vary.
1. graveyard/places where people are buried;
2. mountain, hill; 3. places where they dig up old things

READING STRATEGY: Guessing the Meaning from Context: Using Opposites
○ Go over the information in the box.
○ Ask questions: *What is one way you can guess the meaning of an unfamiliar word? What words might signal that you can use an opposite in the context (but, however, unlike)?*

EXPANSION ACTIVITY: Do It Yourself
○ Model the activity. Write or say a sentence explaining a word from Activity B on page 109 using an opposite (*Some events happen only once, but others may recur frequently*).
○ Have students write sentences using opposites to explain five words from Activity B on page 109.
○ Put students in pairs to share their ideas.
○ Call on students to share their ideas with the class.

C. Vocabulary Preparation: Using Opposites
○ Go over the directions.
○ Have students work in pairs to guess the meanings of the words and phrases.
○ Go over the answers with the class.

ANSWER KEY
1. have only one wife; 2. not large and messy;
3. workers with special ability

Vocabulary Note
○ Prefixes usually change the meaning of a word, often making it negative. Point out or elicit the prefixes that indicate a negative or opposite meaning (*dis-, un-, in-, im-, il-, ir-, ant/anti-*).

D. Vocabulary Preparation: Parts of Speech
○ Go over the directions.
○ Have students circle the parts of speech and write their guesses on the lines.
○ Go over the answers with the class.

ANSWER KEY
Guesses may vary.
1. verb, throw away; 2. noun, places where things are thrown away; 3. verb, learn, discover; 4. noun, discoveries; 5. verb, stays; 6. noun, what was left behind

READING STRATEGY: Recognizing Style: Newspaper Feature Stories

❍ Go over the information in the box.
❍ Ask questions: *What is source material? What is unusual about newspaper style? What are hard news articles? How are feature stories different from hard news articles?*

E. Recognizing Style

❍ Go over the directions with students. Have them look for answers as they read.

ANSWER KEY

There are seven one-sentence paragraphs. Idioms students may find are: *took a toll; played around; put up with.*

🎧 Reading

❍ Go over the directions.
❍ Have students read *Finds Reveal Much of Life at Pyramids* silently, or have them follow along silently as you play the audio program.
❍ Discuss the answers to Activity E on page 112.

ANSWER KEY

The main idea is in the sentence in lines 1–3. Students will differ on what they find interesting in the reading.

Academic Note

❍ Students often overestimate the amount of highlighting that is useful. Point out that students should only highlight about 10–15 percent of what they read.

After Reading

A. Finding the Main Idea

❍ Go over the directions.
❍ Put students in pairs to compare their highlighted sentences.
❍ Go over the answer with the class.

ANSWER KEY

The sentence starting on line 1 is the main idea.

Grammar Note

❍ You may want to point out that simplified grammatical structures are usually used in the headlines and sub-heads of newspaper articles, to save space.

TEST-TAKING STRATEGY: Understanding Idioms

❍ Go over the information in the box.
❍ Ask questions: *What is an idiom? What are some ways you can learn idioms?*

TOEFL® iBT Tip

TOEFL iBT Tip 2: The TOEFL iBT tests the ability to determine the meaning of words in context. Examinees will also be expected to produce sophisticated language in their essays and in the speaking section of the test.

❍ Point out that the test-taking strategy *Understanding Idioms* will help students improve their overall vocabulary for the TOEFL iBT. Idioms are an important component of any language. Understanding and using these expressions is important across all the skill areas of the test—particularly in the integrated reading-listening-writing and listening-reading-speaking tasks.

B. Understanding Idioms
○ Go over the directions.
○ Have students circle the correct meanings of the idioms and then check their answers in pairs.
○ Call on students to share their ideas with the class.

ANSWER KEY
1. D; 2. A, C, B; 3. C, D

C. Word Journal
○ Go over the directions.
○ Have students write words or idioms in their Word Journals.

CRITICAL THINKING STRATEGY: Identifying Causes and Effects
○ Go over the information in the box.
○ Ask questions: *What is another word for* reason? *What is another word for* effect? *What are some cause and effect conjunctions?*

D. Identifying Causes and Effects
○ Go over the directions.
○ Have students draw lines to connect causes and effects.
○ Go over the answers with the class.

ANSWER KEY
1. d; 2. a; 3. e; 4. b; 5. c

TOEFL® iBT Tip

TOEFL iBT Tip 3: The TOEFL iBT may require students to determine the author's rhetorical purpose for a text. This type of question measures the ability to determine why an author uses a particular feature or example in a text.

○ Mention to students that being familiar with cause-effect transition words and conjunctions (*because, so for, since, therefore, thus*) helps them to recognize reasons or purposes stated in a text.

○ Remind students that the ability to recognize transition words and conjunctions can be applied to the answer choices of a rhetorical purpose question and to writing tasks on the test.

On the TOEFL iBT, this question may appear in the following format:
Why does the author introduce the claim that . . .?

EXPANSION ACTIVITY: Matching Slips
○ Photocopy the Black Line Master *Cause and Effect Matching* on page BLM 8. Cut along the dotted lines.
○ Give each student a strip of paper. Have students stand and walk around the classroom, talking to each other in order to match each cause and effect.
○ Have students stand with the classmate who has the matching strip.
○ Ask students to read their strips aloud.
○ For variation, make enough photocopies so that each pair of students has a set of strips. Have them work in pairs to match the strips.

E. Making Inferences
○ Go over the directions.
○ Have students write specific information in the article to support each inference.
○ Students compare ideas with a partner.
○ Go over the answers with the class.

ANSWER KEY
1. Lines 1–3; Life wasn't all work and no play.
2. Lines 23–25: deaths from injuries, bent spines
3. Lines 47–54: skilled workers, foremen, workers

EXPANSION ACTIVITY: Correct or Incorrect?

○ Model the activity. Say a statement about the information in the article (*The man found between his wife and his girlfriend was lower class.*). Elicit whether the inference is correct or incorrect and why (*Correct: The last statement says upper-class people avoided such scandal.*).

○ Have students write three inferences based on the information. Remind them to make some true and some false.

○ Put students in pairs to challenge each other.

○ Call on students to read their statements to the class and elicit if the inference is correct or incorrect.

PART ❸ ACADEMIC READING
EGYPTIAN CIVILIZATION: A BRIEF HISTORY, PAGES 117–124

Before Reading

A. Thinking Ahead

○ Go over the directions.
○ Have students discuss the questions in small groups.
○ Call on students to share their ideas with the class.

ANSWER KEY

Answers may vary.
Art was still of rulers and the most important people. Art was less stiff and more realistic. Art showed rulers alone, not surrounded by others. Art depicted figures straight on, not in profile.

B. Vocabulary Preparation

○ Go over the directions.
○ Have students match the definitions with the words or phrases and then compare their answers with a partner.
○ Go over the answers with the class.

ANSWER KEY

1. d; 2. c; 3. b; 4. a; 5. e; 6. g; 7. f

EXPANSION ACTIVITY: Tell a Story

○ Have students tell a story using all the words in Activity B. Point out that the story could be a fairy tale, a modern story, or history. Encourage students to write the story down first so they can remember it.

○ Put students in pairs to tell their stories.

○ Call on students to share their stories with the class.

Reading

○ Go over the directions before the reading. Read the question aloud.

○ Have students read *Egyptian Civilization: A Brief History* silently, or play the audio program and have students follow along silently.

○ Elicit answers to the question from the class.

Culture Note

○ The Hyksos invaded Egypt using chariots as well as bronze weapons. They may have come from Canaan and Phoenicia, and they first established themselves in Avaris and then Memphis. The Hyksos were relatively benign rulers who respected the Egyptian culture and religion, and formed the 15th and 16th dynasties of Egypt.

Pronunciation Notes

○ You may want to point out that when a word ends in a -*y* and the next word begins with a vowel, we join the *y* sound to the vowel sound.

○ In this reading, there are several such phrases (*by a, body of, They easily*).

EXPANSION ACTIVITY: Mark Joinings

○ Play the audio program for *Egyptian Civilization: A Brief History*.

○ Have students use a curved line ⌒ to indicate when the consonant sound from one word joins the vowel sound in the next.

○ Have students compare their marked texts in pairs.

○ Call on students to tell the class about a phrase they marked.

After Reading

A. Finding Details

○ Go over the directions.
○ Have students complete the chart.
○ Put students in pairs to discuss their charts. Call on students to share their ideas with the class.

ANSWER KEY

	Old Kingdom (c. 3100 B.C.E.)	Middle Kingdom (c. 2040 B.C.E.)	New Kingdom (c. 1570 B.C.E.)
Historical Events	Menes founded the first dynasty	foreign armies took over Egypt for 200 years difficult period for Egypt	great military power Ikhnaton changed the religion and capital Golden Age of Egypt Tutankhamen became king
Art Associated with the Period	pyramids began to create *ka* statues	stopped building pyramids tombs in rock cliffs portraits surprisingly realistic and sad	rules for artists became more relaxed

B. Vocabulary Check

○ Go over the directions.
○ Have students write the correct words on the lines and then check their answers with a partner.
○ Go over the answers with the class.

ANSWER KEY

1. dynasty; 2. found; 3. massive; 4. treasures;
5. chariots

READING STRATEGY: Guessing the Meaning from Context: *in other words, that is, i.e.*

○ Go over the information in the box.

C. Guessing the Meaning from Context

○ Go over the directions.
○ Have students answer the questions in pairs.
○ Go over the answers with the class.

ANSWER KEY

1. a commoner; 2. a high official, similar to a prime minister; 3. a person with no royal blood

EXPANSION ACTIVITY: In Other Words

○ Have students write sentences explaining the words from Activity B by using the expressions from the reading strategy (*in other words, that is, i.e.*).

READING STRATEGY: Finding Evidence

○ Go over the information in the box.
○ Ask questions: *What is a theory? What is evidence?*

D. Finding Evidence

○ Go over the directions.
○ Have students answer the questions in small groups.
○ Go over the answers with the class.

ANSWER KEY

1. The theory is that Tutankhamen was murdered.
2. Evidence: a letter in which Ankhesenamen writes that she doesn't want to marry a commoner (possibly the vizier) and she is afraid; the vizier did succeed Tut; and a ring that suggests the vizier and Ankhesenamen were married
3. Answers will vary.
4. Answers will vary.

CHAPTER 4 • The Ancient World: Egypt • 55

TOEFL® iBT Tip

TOEFL iBT Tip 4: The TOEFL iBT requires examinees to recognize minor, less important ideas that do not belong in a summary; or, distinguish between major and minor points or information.

❍ Point out that the reading strategy for *Finding Evidence* will help students distinguish between major and minor points in a text on the TOEFL iBT. It will also help them differentiate between supporting details for the argument that an author is trying to make or the opinion the author is trying to support.

❍ Explain to students that one type of question that appears on the test is called a prose summary or classification question. Partial credit is given for correct answers to this question type and the answers are not in traditional multiple-choice format. The question type appears in the form of a schematic table that requires examinees to select and drag answer choices to specific positions in a chart.

❍ Being able to find evidence to support a theory, opinion, or argument will help students master this question type on the test and will enhance their writing skills.

E. Word Journal
❍ Go over the directions.
❍ Have students write words in their Word Journals.

F. Pronoun Reference
❍ Go over the directions.
❍ Have students circle the noun or noun phrase the pronoun refers to.
❍ Go over the answers with the class.

ANSWER KEY
1. *ka*; 2. Thieves; 3. Sculptors; 4. daughters

G. Identifying Causes and Effects
❍ Go over the directions.
❍ Have students answer the questions and then compare answers with a partner.
❍ Go over the answers with the class.

ANSWER KEY
1. It was important to keep the blood of the royal family pure.
2. If the body was destroyed, the *ka* had to travel aimlessly for all eternity.
3. Thieves broke into the pyramids, stole the gold, and destroyed the pharaoh's body.
4. The Egyptians were fighting on foot, and the Hyksos had horses and chariots.

H. Analysis
❍ Go over the directions.
❍ Have students complete the chart and then discuss their charts in small groups.
❍ Call on students to share their ideas with the class.

ANSWER KEY
Answers may vary.

Elements	Wall Painting from the Tomb of Nebamun
Time (year and period—which kingdom?)	1450 B.C.E., New Kingdom
Use of space	Space is filled in with plants, birds, people, fish
Other figures or animals	Small figure between central figure's legs; also a woman on the right, many birds, several fish
Central figure (pose, size, actions, style)	Stiff standing figure; head and legs seen in profile, torso and one eye seen from the front.
Adjectives to describe this work of art	(Answers will vary.)

Website Research

○ For additional information on Egyptian art, refer students to these websites:
  • Lisa Kremen, Understanding Egyptian Art
    http://www.bergen.org/AAST/Projects/Egypt/
    egyptian_art.html
  • Detroit Institute of Arts
    http://www.dia.org/collections/ancient/egypt/
    egypt.html
  • University of Memphis, Egyptian Artifacts Exhibit
    http://academic.memphis.edu/egypt//
    artifact.html
  • Metropolitan Museum of Art, The Art of Ancient Egypt
    http://www.metmuseum.org/explore/newegypt/
    htm/a_index.htm
  • Emory University, Ancient Egyptian Art
    http://www.carlos.emory.edu/collection/egypt/

PART THE MECHANICS OF WRITING, PAGES 125–129

○ Go over the information about Part 4.

TOEFL® iBT Tip

TOEFL iBT Tip 5: The TOEFL iBT does not discretely test grammar skills. However, examinees' essay scores will be based on the range of grammar and vocabulary used in their essays.

○ Point out that the grammar activities in *The Mechanics of Writing* part of this chapter will help them improve their use of conjunctions and transitions for cause-effect essay writing.

○ Remind students that being able to recognize these grammatical structures and use them appropriately in their essays will improve their overall reading and writing skills.

Infinitives of Purpose

○ Go over the information in the box about infinitives of purpose.
○ Ask comprehension questions: *What is an infinitive? What question does an infinitive of purpose answer?*

A. Infinitives of Purpose

○ Go over the directions and the example.
○ Have students match the phrases with the purposes and then write complete sentences using infinitives of purpose.
○ Have students compare sentences in pairs.
○ Go over the answers with the class.

ANSWER KEY

The position of clauses may vary.
1. b; 2. c; 3. a; 4. d; 5. e
  1. Mix blue and yellow to make green. (To make green, mix blue and yellow.)
  2. Mix red and yellow to make orange.
  3. Use plants, animals, and hieroglyphs to fill empty space.
  4. Make the pharaoh larger than other figures to show his importance.
  5. There should be servants in tomb art to take care of pharaohs for eternity.

EXPANSION ACTIVITY: *Why* Questions

○ Model the activity. Ask a *why* question (*Why are you taking this class?*) and elicit answers with infinitives of purpose (*I'm taking this class to improve my English.*).
○ Have students write five *why* questions to ask a classmate.
○ Put students in pairs to take turns asking and answering questions. Remind students to use infinitives of purpose in their answers.
○ Call on students to share their answers with the class.

Transitional Expressions of Cause and Effect: Subordinating Conjunctions

○ Go over the information in the box.
○ Ask: *What are some subordinating conjunctions that show cause and effect? When do we use a comma?*

B. Sentence Combining: Subordinating Conjunctions

○ Go over the directions.
○ Have students combine the pairs of sentences.
○ Have students compare sentences in pairs.
○ Call on students to read their sentences to the class.

ANSWER KEY

1. a. Art historians now know more about the lives of the pyramid builders because/since/as archaeologists have been excavating the workers' tombs.
   b. Because/Since/As archaeologists have been excavating the workers' tombs, art historians now know more about the lives of the pyramid builders.
2. a. Because/Since/As many people had thought that the pyramid builders were all slaves, they were surprised.
   b. Many people were surprised because/since/as they had thought that the pyramid builders were all slaves.
3. a. Expert opinion is that pyramid builders did not all have the same status because/since/as they had tombs of different quality.
   b. Because/Since/As pyramid builders had tombs of different quality, expert opinion is that they did not all have the same status.

Transitional Expressions and Phrases

○ Go over the information in the box.
○ Ask: *What expressions are used with causes that are nouns or noun phrases?*

C. Transitional Expressions

○ Go over the directions.
○ Have students complete the paragraph with transitional expressions of cause and effect.
○ Have students compare their ideas in small groups.
○ Call on students to share their ideas with the class.

ANSWER KEY

Answers will vary.
1. Because of/Due to; 2. because/since/as;
3. because/since/as; 4. Because of/Due to;
5. because/since/as

Conjunctions of Cause and Effect: Review

○ Go over the information in the box.
○ Ask questions: *Why should you know and use a variety of expressions to express cause and effect? Which ones are used to join two main clauses? Which ones are used with subordinating clauses?*

D. Review: Conjunctions of Cause and Effect

○ Go over the directions.
○ Have students rewrite each sentence in two different ways, using the conjunction in parentheses.
○ Have students compare their sentences in pairs.
○ Go over the answers with the class.

ANSWER KEY

1. a. Workers had bent spines, for they carried heavy stone blocks.
   b. Workers carried heavy stone blocks; therefore, they had bent spines.
2. a. Some workers had higher status than other workers, so they were buried in tombs at the top of the cliffside cemetery.
   b. Some workers had higher status than other workers; for this reason, they were buried in tombs at the top of the cliffside cemetery.
3. a. Some workers were buried at the bottom of the cliffside cemetery, for they had lower status than others.
   b. Some workers had lower status than others; consequently, they were buried at the bottom of the cliffside cemetery.
4. a. Many workers suffered accidents and injuries, so they died quite young.
   b. Many workers suffered accidents and injuries; as a result, they died quite young.
5. a. The upper classes avoided "playing around" since they were in the public eye.
   b. The upper classes were in the public eye; therefore, they avoided "playing around."

E. Review: Finding Errors

○ Go over the directions.
○ Have students circle the letter under the incorrect word or phrase.
○ Go over the answers with the class. Have students explain what the errors are and how to correct them.

ANSWER KEY

1. B; 2. C; 3. C; 4. B; 5. C

EXPANSION ACTIVITY: Editing Practice

○ Photocopy and distribute the Black Line Master *Editing Practice* on BLM 9.
○ Have students correct the paragraph and then compare ideas with a partner.
○ Go over the answers with the class.

ANSWER KEY

Ancient Egyptians spent vast amounts of time and wealth on huge magnificent tombs ^to^ protect their dead kings/^^ however, grave robbers managed to break into most tombs and steal the fabulous contents. Therefore^ there was tremendous excitement when the tomb of Tutankhamen was discovered in 1922. The tomb had not been robbed, and as a result ^ it was still filled with an almost unimaginable number of priceless objects, including the (gold) astonishing mask of the pharaoh himself. The richness of the tomb was also surprising because ~~of~~ "King Tut" ~~he~~ was just eighteen years old when he died and ~~that~~ he was considered a Egyptian minor king.

PART 5 ACADEMIC WRITING, PAGES 130–133

Writing Assignment

○ Go over the writing assignment.
○ Have students read the five steps.
○ Direct students' attention to Step A and then to the art on page 124.

TEST-TAKING STRATEGY: Applying Information

○ Go over the information in the box.
○ Ask: *What is the instructor trying to find out in an essay exam? What types of essay exams are there? Which is the most common? What should you do before you begin writing?*

○ Direct students' attention to Step B. Go over the directions and the steps. Have students list the elements of the figures and the reasons for the elements. Then tell them to write down any information about the history of the period that can help them understand more about the painting.

TOEFL® iBT Tip

TOEFL iBT Tip 6: The integrated writing skill on the TOEFL iBT requires students to think critically about material that they have read, interpret that information, relate it to a lecture, and then present ideas in essay format.

○ Point out that the *Writing a Paragraph of Cause and Effect* activity corresponds to a strategy they will need to use when writing their independent or integrated essays. They will often be given two ideas and be asked to argue for or against one of those ideas or show a relationship between the ideas presented.

○ The process writing approach will help students organize their thoughts and take meaningful steps toward developing their essays.

WRITING STRATEGY: Writing a Paragraph of Cause and Effect

○ Go over the information in the box.

○ Ask comprehension questions: *What words can signal a cause and effect essay question? What do you often have to do in an art history class?*

○ You may want to read the example paragraph aloud as students follow silently in their books.

○ Go over the points for students to notice in the example.

○ Read the *Analysis* directions. Ask students to highlight the transition words of cause and effect and purpose.

○ Go over answers with the class.

ANSWER KEY

The figures on Tutankhamen's magnificent throne seem somewhat unnatural to the modern observer <u>because</u> the artist was following the strict rules for artists in ancient Egypt. These figures are depictions of the pharaoh and his queen<u>, so</u> they appear inactive and unmoving <u>to show</u> their high status. <u>Since</u> the queen's figure is the same size as her husband's, we can assume that she was considered his equal in status. Egyptian religion required artists to depict all parts of the body from the most familiar point of view. <u>Consequently,</u> we see the feet, arms, and head of these figures in profile and their shoulders and eye from the front. Also, arms and legs of both people are clearly shown so that their *ka* can live forever in a complete body. This throne was created in the New Kingdom. <u>As a result,</u> it is clear that there is some influence from the naturalness of art at that time. For example, both figures appear less stiff, less frozen than most figures in earlier periods of Egyptian art.

CRITICAL THINKING STRATEGY: Evaluating

Evaluating is an important critical thinking strategy. In this writing assignment, students will evaluate a piece of art, describing and assessing how certain elements are portrayed.

○ Direct students' attention to Step C. Go over the directions and have students write their paragraphs.

○ Direct students' attention to Step D. Go over the questions. Have students read and edit their paragraphs using the questions as a guide.

○ For peer editing, have students exchange paragraphs with a partner, edit, and return to the writer.

○ Go over the directions for Step E. Have students carefully rewrite their paragraphs and hand them in to you.

○ After you have read and returned students' paragraphs, you may want to set aside time for students to read each other's writing or display the paragraphs in the classroom. Have students keep all of their final versions in a notebook or folder so that they can see their progress and improvement over time.

EXPANSION ACTIVITY: Presentations

○ Bring in art books with large color illustrations or direct students to the websites on page 53 of this book. Students can work individually, in pairs, or in small groups to discuss a painting, the reasons for how the space is used, and the figures depicted.

○ Discuss with students what should be included in a visual presentation in contrast to a written paper. Stress the importance of having interesting visuals in the presentation and the importance of looking at the audience while speaking (rather than reading notes or a paper).

○ Have students practice giving their presentations to each other. Remind them to give the names of the pieces of art and the time frame. Give students a two-minute time limit to keep the presentations short and manageable.

○ Ask for volunteers to give their presentations to the class.

Unit 2 Vocabulary Workshop

Have students review vocabulary from Chapters 3 and 4.

A. Matching
○ Go over the directions.
○ Have students match definitions with words or phrases.

ANSWER KEY
1. j; 2. g; 3. c; 4. a; 5. f; 6. b; 7. e; 8. h; 9. i; 10. d

B. True or False?
○ Go over the directions.
○ Have students fill in the bubbles.

ANSWER KEY
1. F; 2. T; 3. T; 4. T; 5. F; 6. T; 7. F; 8. F

C. Odd One Out
○ Go over the directions.
○ Have students cross out the word that doesn't belong.

ANSWER KEY
1. scribe; 2. abolitionist; 3. falcon; 4. spiritual; 5. hut; 6. journey; 7. surround; 8. change

D. Vocabulary Expansion
○ Go over the directions.
○ Have students complete the chart.

ANSWER KEY

	Verbs	Nouns	Adjectives
1.	describe	description	descriptive
2.	analyze	analysis	analytical
3.	excavate	excavation	excavated
4.	stabilize	stability	stable
5.	find/found	foundation	founded
6.	animate	animation	animated
7.	rule	ruler	ruling
8.	establish	establishment	established

E. The Academic Word List
○ Go over the directions.
○ Have students write the words on the lines.

ANSWER KEY
1. abstract; 2. contrast; 3. principal; 4. philosopher; 5. features; 6. so-called; 7. created; 8. illustrates; 9. indicate; 10. status; 11. section; 12. pose; 13. established; 14. maintained; 15. stability; 16. goals

Unit Opener, page 137

○ Direct students' attention to the picture on page 137. Ask questions: *What do you see? How is this picture related to the unit topic?*

○ Write *psychology* on the board and help students brainstorm words related to psychology. Ask: *What topics do you think will be in this unit?* Circle the words they suggest.

CHAPTER 5 STATES OF CONSCIOUSNESS

In Part 1 of this chapter, students will read about lucid dreaming. In Part 2, they will read about dreaming in different cultures. In Part 3, students will learn about the function and meaning of dreaming. Part 4 focuses on the mechanics of writing, including transition words of time and tenses in narration. Students will also apply the strategy of writing about symbols. Finally, in Part 5, students will write two paragraphs: the first a narrative of a dream and the second an analysis of that dream.

VOCABULARY

at random	dream catcher	ill will	nightmare	seek
carve	drill	in a panic	objective	significance
colleagues	folk belief	key	overt	spell
critical	fulfill	latent	plausible	subjective
cure	guide	lucid dreaming	REM sleep	sufficient
disguise	heal	manifest	sacrifice	vision

READING STRATEGIES

Understanding Ellipses
Having Questions in Mind
Finding the Topic Sentence
Choosing the Correct Dictionary Definition

CRITICAL THINKING STRATEGIES

Thinking Ahead (Parts 1, 2, and 3)
Determining Point of View (Part 1)
Making Connections (Part 2)
Analysis (Part 5)
Note: The strategy in bold is highlighted in the student book.

MECHANICS

Using Transition Words of Time
Using Verbs in Narration

WRITING STRATEGIES

Writing About Symbols
Gathering and Organizing Ideas
Using Graphic Organizers: Idea Maps
Writing a Paragraph of Analysis

TEST-TAKING STRATEGY

Answering Questions about Details

CHAPTER 5 States of Consciousness

Chapter 5 Opener, page 139
- ○ Direct students' attention to the chapter title and photo. Read the questions aloud.
- ○ Put students in pairs or small groups to discuss the questions.
- ○ Call on students to share their ideas with the class.

PART 1 INTRODUCTION
LUCID DREAMING, PAGES 140–143

EXPANSION ACTIVITY: Pair Interview
- ○ Write this question on the board: *What is the last dream you remember having?*
- ○ Model the activity. Describe a dream you remember having recently. Tell students that they can also talk about a dream they remember from the past. Often students will remember a nightmare they have had.
- ○ Put students in pairs to take turns describing one of their recent dreams.
- ○ Call on students to tell the class about their partner's dream.

Before Reading
Thinking Ahead
- ○ Have students look at the ads on page 140.
- ○ Go over the directions and questions.
- ○ Have students discuss the questions in pairs.
- ○ Call on students to share their ideas with the class.

ANSWER KEY
Answers may vary.
1. Lucid dreaming is knowing when you are dreaming and directing the dream.
2. Someone might buy a dream catcher to prevent nightmares or so they would have good dreams.

🎧 Reading
- ○ Have students look at the reading. Direct their attention to the two section titles to help them anticipate content.
- ○ Go over the directions and the questions.
- ○ Have students read silently, or have students follow along silently as you play the audio program.

Culture Notes
- ○ Aristotle was a Greek philosopher and writer who lived from 384 B.C.E. to 322 B.C.E.
- ○ Oliver Fox was born in 1885 and suffered from nightmares as a child. He went on to experiment with dreaming and projection.

CRITICAL THINKING STRATEGY: Making Connections
Making connections is an important critical thinking strategy. Remind students that they can understand and remember a text better when they make connections between it and something they already know.

EXPANSION ACTIVITY: Text Connections
- ○ Photocopy and distribute the Black Line Master *Text Connections* on page BLM 10.
- ○ Explain that we often make connections between a text and our own experience (text to self), between one text and another (text to text), and between a text and something we know about the world (text to world).
- ○ Have students read *Lucid Dreaming* and jot down any connections in the appropriate places on the chart.
- ○ Put students in pairs to talk about their ideas.
- ○ Call on students to share their ideas with the class.

ANSWER KEY
Answers will vary.

After Reading

A. Check Your Understanding

❍ Go over the directions.
❍ Have students highlight the sentences in the reading that answer the questions.
❍ Go over the answers with the class.

ANSWER KEY

Answers may vary, but students should highlight information in the following lines:
1. lines 15–21
2. lines 34–41

CRITICAL THINKING STRATEGY: Determining Point of View

❍ Go over the information in the box.
❍ Ask comprehension questions: *What is the difference between an objective passage and a subjective passage? What are some examples of adjectives of opinion?*

B. Determining Point of View

❍ Go over the directions.
❍ Have students discuss the question in pairs.
❍ Go over the answers with the class.

ANSWER KEY

The author believes that it is good to be a lucid dreamer. He uses adjectives such as *special, unbelievable,* and *positive.* He encourages the reader to try lucid dreaming and gives instructions. He ends with a wish: *Good journeying.*

TOEFL® iBT Tip

TOEFL iBT Tip 1: The TOEFL iBT tests the ability to make inferences or draw conclusions based on what is implied in a passage. In some questions, examinees may be required to demonstrate an understanding of why an author explains concepts in a certain way.

❍ Point out that the strategy for *Determining Point of View* requires students to draw conclusions and form generalizations based on information presented in the reading. Recognizing an author's use of adjectives or descriptions is a good way to determine his or her point of view.

On the TOEFL iBT, this question may appear in the following format:
Why does the author state _____?

READING STRATEGY: Understanding Ellipses

❍ Go over the information in the box.
❍ Ask: *What are ellipses? When do we use them?*

C. Understanding Ellipses

❍ Go over the directions.
❍ Have students find and circle the ellipses.
❍ Ask students why the ellipses were used.

ANSWER KEY

Students should circle ellipses in lines 5, 6, 10, 16, and 19. The ellipses are used to show that some words from the original quote have been left out.

D. Taking a Survey

❍ Go over the directions. Depending on the size of your class, you can either have students interview every student, set a number of students to interview, or set a time limit.
❍ Have students stand and walk around the classroom to interview classmates.

E. Discussion
- ○ Go over the directions.
- ○ Put students in small groups to talk about the survey results from Activity D.
- ○ Call on students to share their ideas with the class.

EXPANSION ACTIVITY: Graph It
- ○ Reproduce the Activity D chart on the board.
- ○ Ask the questions; students respond by raising their hands. For each answer, tally the class results on the chart. For example, ask, *Do you remember your dreams? How many people say "No, never?" How many say "Rarely?"*
- ○ Have students select one of the questions to graph answers for.
- ○ Show how to make a bar graph. Write the total number of students on the vertical axis, and write the responses across the bottom of the horizontal axis. See the example below.

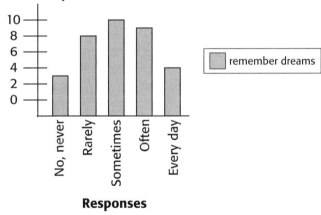

- ○ Have students create bar graphs in small groups.

F. Application
- ○ Go over the directions.
- ○ Have students record their dreams in a notebook. Encourage students to write down anything they can remember, even if it is just a few words. With practice and motivation, they will become better at remembering their dreams. Remind students they may use these notes in their writing assignment at the end of the chapter.

PART ② GENERAL INTEREST READING
DREAMING ACROSS CULTURES, PAGES 144–148

Before Reading
A. Thinking Ahead
- ○ Go over the directions and the questions.
- ○ Have students work in small groups to discuss the questions.
- ○ Call on students to share their ideas with the class.

ANSWER KEY
Answers will vary.

B. Vocabulary Preparation
- ○ Go over the directions.
- ○ Read the first sentence aloud. Elicit possible completions.
- ○ Have students work in pairs to write definitions.
- ○ Go over the answers with the class.

ANSWER KEY
Answers may vary.
1. cut wood; 2. cured/made better/healthy; 3. killed;
4. treatment/solution; 5. looking for/searching for;
6. show us the way

EXPANSION ACTIVITY: Word Families
- ○ Have students work in pairs to generate other words with the same base words from Activity B.
- ○ Call on students to share their ideas with the class. Have students identify the part of speech for each word in the word families.
- ○ Point out to students that the opposite of *curable* is *incurable,* a common word related to health.
- ○ Encourage students to add words to their Word Journals.

ANSWER KEY

carve: carving
heal: health, healthy, healer
sacrifice: sacrificial, sacrificially
cure: curable
seek: seeker
guide: guidance

READING STRATEGY: Having Questions in Mind

○ Go over the information in the box.
○ Ask: *Why is it a good idea to have questions in mind before you read? Often questions come at the end of a reading. How does previewing these questions help you read?*

🎧 Reading

○ Go over the directions and read aloud the questions in Activity A on page 147.
○ Have students read *Dreaming Across Cultures* silently, or have them follow along silently as you play the audio program.
○ Remind students to look for the answers to the questions on page 147 and highlight information and answers as they read.

Culture Notes

○ The Poro Society is a male secret society in the Senufo culture of the Cote D'Ivoire and Mali. The Poro try to maintain good relationships between the living world and the ancestors while keeping witches away.
○ The *malanggan* ceremony is in honor of ancestors, but is also an initiation ceremony for young men.
○ Edward Tylor lived from 1832 to 1917. He was a professor of anthropology at Oxford University in England and studied the religions of primitive peoples.
○ Peyote has been used by Native American tribes in Mexico and Texas for thousands of years, but its use spread to other parts of the United States after the Civil War. It is used by some people in the Native American Church because it is believed to bring users closer to God.

After Reading

A. Comprehension Check

○ Go over the directions.
○ Have students review the reading and any sentences they highlighted to answer the questions.
○ Have students compare answers in small groups.
○ Go over the answers with the class.

ANSWER KEY

1. The Christians and Greeks were similar in that they both thought that dreams would help them to be healthy. Both also believed the gods or God might speak to them in their dreams. Greeks sacrificed an animal first and then would sleep in the temple in order to dream. You could infer that the Church did not approve of the Christians sleeping in the church because it did not want people to use dreams as a way to communicate directly with God; this could lessen the power of the Church.
2. Some Native Americans use peyote or a vision quest to have special visions. Peyote is a drug that can bring on visions. On a vision quest, the Native Americans suffer hunger, physical pain, and loneliness for several days in an attempt to have a vision.

B. Making Connections

○ Go over the directions.
○ Have students discuss the question and then explain their answers in pairs.
○ Call on students to share their ideas with the class.

ANSWER KEY

The Senoi seem to be the best example of a culture that practices lucid dreaming. They tell each other their dreams, and then they learn to use their dreams creatively. Their goal is for dreamers to gain control of their dream world. Other cultures use dream images and visions to guide their lives but do not try to participate in their dreams or direct them.

READING STRATEGY: Finding the Topic Sentence

❍ Go over the information in the box.
❍ Ask questions: *Why is the first sentence sometimes not a good topic sentence? What is an "umbrella" sentence?*

C. Finding the Topic Sentence

❍ Go over the directions. Have students number the paragraphs from 1 to 7 for easy reference.
❍ Have students find and highlight the topic sentences.
❍ Have students compare ideas in small groups.
❍ Call on students to share their ideas with the class.

ANSWER KEY

In Paragraphs 3 and 4, the topic sentence is the first sentence.
Paragraph 1: Topic sentence is the second sentence: *Tylor believed that "primitive" early humans developed the idea of a soul from their attempts to explain dreaming.*
Paragraph 2: Topic sentence is the second sentence: *Artists in very different cultures receive inspiration for their art from dreams.*
Paragraph 5: Topic sentence is the second sentence: *European Christians used to sleep in churches in the hopes of having a dream to cure their sickness.*
Paragraph 6: Topic sentence is the second sentence: *Traditionally, they used their dreams to control their waking life.*
Paragraph 7: Topic sentence is the second sentence: *Native Americans in North America who follow their people's traditions may seek a vision—a rare and special kind of dream—in two ways: through the use of peyote or through a vision quest.*

TOEFL® iBT Tip

TOEFL iBT Tip 2: The TOEFL iBT does not directly test the ability to determine the main idea in a text. Instead, examinees are required to recognize the minor, less important ideas that do not belong in a summary; or, they may be required to distinguish between major and minor points of information.

❍ Point out that the strategy for *Finding the Topic Sentence* will help students distinguish between major and minor points in a text on the TOEFL iBT and link those ideas throughout the passage.

❍ Remind students that this will also help them with more challenging question types and sentence simplification questions, where they must be able to locate information and position a sentence where it belongs, or recognize and create accurate paraphrases of information from a reading passage.

D. Identifying General and Specific Ideas

❍ Go over the directions.
❍ Have students complete the chart and then compare answers in small groups.
❍ Call on students to share their ideas with the class. Discuss the importance of supporting general ideas with specific examples.

ANSWER KEY

Answers may vary. See ideas below.

Group of People	How Dreams Are/Were Used or Understood (main ideas)	Examples or Details
Artists	For inspiration	Poro society masks malanggan ceremony
Egyptians	Lucky or unlucky	Go to a priest for interpretation

ANSWER KEY, continued

Greeks/ Medieval Christians	Guide to health	Greeks sacrificed animal; slept on floor of temple Christians slept in church; Church didn't like it because it lessened its power
Senoi	To control their waking life; to change feelings of ill will into good will	Meet and discuss dreams at breakfast Nightmare about falling interpreted as way to contact spirit world Dream of attack—needed to apologize to that person
Native Americans	For guidance	Dreams with peyote Vision quest Visions associated with images from their cultures (Mexican—bird; Indian from flatlands—buffalo)

E. Vocabulary Check

○ Go over the directions. Remind students that definitions and clues to a word's meaning are often set apart with parentheses or dashes.
○ Have students write the words on the lines.
○ Go over the answers with the class.

ANSWER KEY

1. spell; 2. having; 3. ill will

PART ③ ACADEMIC READING
THE FUNCTION AND MEANING OF DREAMING, PAGES 149–156

Before Reading

A. Thinking Ahead
○ Go over the directions.
○ Have students discuss the question in small groups.
○ Call on students to share their ideas with the class.

ANSWER KEY

Answers will vary.

B. Vocabulary Preparation
○ Go over the directions.
○ Have students write their guesses on the lines and then compare their answers with a partner.
○ Go over the answers with the class.

ANSWER KEY

Answers may vary.
1. very worried, in a great hurry; 2. makes holes in; 3. importance, meaning; 4. satisfy, achieve; 5. dressed up as, pretended to be; 6. obvious, visible; 7. by chance; 8. enough; 9. other professors; 10. possible, sensible, logical

---

EXPANSION ACTIVITY: Beanbag Toss

○ Give students one minute to review the new words in Activity B.
○ Call on a student and toss a ball or beanbag as you say one of the new words. Elicit its meaning from the student.
○ Have the student call on a classmate, toss the ball or beanbag, and say a new word.
○ Continue until everyone has had a chance to participate. As a variation, students can say the definition and elicit the new word.

READING STRATEGY: Choosing the Correct Dictionary Definition

○ Go over the information in the box.
○ Ask questions: *Do most words have just one meaning? How do you know which dictionary definition is the right one? What can help you to find the right definition? In the example, what part of speech is* vision?

C. Vocabulary Preparation: Dictionary Use

○ Go over the directions.
○ Have students make guesses about the words and then check the definitions in the dictionary.
○ Call on students to tell the class how close their guess was to the dictionary definition.

ANSWER KEY

Student guesses will vary. Here are possible dictionary definitions:
critical: very important
key: very important, essential
works out to: amounts to a total

EXPANSION ACTIVITY: Preview Questions

○ Have students preview the reading, noticing the art, captions, and headings. Point out that a different typeface (font) is used for the first paragraph because it is an extended excerpt or quote.
○ Ask students to work in pairs and to list three questions they have about the material. Ask: *What do you want to learn about dreaming? What questions do you have about dreaming?*
○ As students read, have them highlight any answers to their questions.
○ After they have read the text, call on students to tell which questions they found answers for.

Reading

○ Go over the directions before the reading. Read the questions aloud.
○ Have students read *The Function and Meaning of Dreaming* silently, or play the audio program and have students follow along silently.
○ Elicit answers to the questions from the class.

Culture Notes

○ Sigmund Freud was an Austrian physician who lived between 1856 and 1939. He was the founder of psychoanalysis.
○ M. C. Escher was a Dutch graphic artist who was born at the end of the 19th century. He is best known for using interlocking patterns and creating optical illusions.
○ J. Allan Hobson is the director of the Neuro-physiology and Sleep Laboratory and professor of psychiatry at Harvard Medical School. He wrote *Dreaming: A Very Short Introduction* in 2005.
○ Paul Nash was a British landscape painter who focused on the time period of World War I. Near the end of his life, his art became increasingly abstract and surreal, as shown in the painting.

Pronunciation Notes: Thought Groups

○ Native speakers pause between thought groups, or groups of words that form a single idea. Written English marks thought groups with punctuation such as periods, commas, colons, semicolons, and dashes.
○ Your students may have an easier time comprehending a reading if they can read it with the correct intonation and pausing. Point out that native speakers don't simply say words faster; they say a group of words together, pause slightly, and continue. Have students listen for thought groups as they listen to the reading on the audio program.

EXPANSION ACTIVITY: Marking Thought Groups
○ Play the audio program again and have students put a slash (/) where they hear the reader pause.
○ Ask students what types of phrases form thought groups (*prepositional phrases, clauses, appositives, long noun phrases, or verb and object combinations*).
○ Explain that punctuation often marks thought groups.

After Reading

A. Finding Main Ideas
○ Go over the directions.
○ Have students complete the chart.
○ Put students in pairs to discuss their charts. Call on students to share their ideas with the class.

ANSWER KEY

Theory	Person(s) Associated with This Theory	Main Ideas of This Theory
Unconscious wish fulfill-ment	Freud	Dreams are unconscious wishes dreamers want to fulfill
Dreams-for-Survival		Dreams permit information that is critical to our daily survival to be reconsidered and reprocessed.
Activation-Synthesis	J. Allan Hobson	Electrical stimula-tion of memories in brain creates images—we create the storyline.
New research	e.g., Allen Braun	Parts of brain associated with emotions and visual imagery are strongly activated during REM sleep (may support Freud)

B. Vocabulary Check
○ Go over the directions.
○ Have students write the correct words on the lines and then check their answers with a partner.
○ Go over the answers with the class.

ANSWER KEY
1. nightmares; 2. latent content of dreams; 3. manifest content (of dreams); 4. REM

Vocabulary Notes
○ The prefix *psych* is from the Greek *psukho-* meaning soul or life. This prefix is used in many common words, such as *psychologist, psyche, psychedelic, psychosomatic,* and *psychotic* to name a few.
○ A *psychologist* is a person who has completed a doctorate in psychology. A *psychiatrist* is a medical doctor with a specialization in psychiatry. Both can use the title *Doctor.*

C. Word Journal
○ Go over the directions.
○ Have students write words in their Word Journals.

TEST-TAKING STRATEGY: Answering Questions About Details
○ Go over the information in the box.

TOEFL® iBT Tip

TOEFL iBT Tip 3: The TOEFL iBT tests the ability to understand key facts and the important information contained within a text. The strategy *Answering Questions About Details* helps students build vocabulary and improve their reading skills.

○ Point out that the reading section of the TOEFL iBT may require examinees to identify information that is *not* included in the passage.

○ The *Answering Questions About Details* activity will help to scaffold students' abilities upward toward mastering the negative fact questions on the test.

On the TOEFL iBT, this question may appear in the following format:

All of the following are mentioned in paragraph ___ as _____ EXCEPT . . .

D. Answering Questions About Details
○ Go over the directions.
○ Have students circle the correct answer.
○ Go over the answers with the class.

ANSWER KEY
1. A; 2. D; 3. B

E. Discussion
○ Go over the directions.
○ Have students discuss the questions in small groups.
○ Call on students to share their ideas with the class.

ANSWER KEY
Answers will vary.

F. Application
○ Go over the directions.
○ Have students work in pairs to analyze the dreams.
○ Call on students to share their ideas with the class.

ANSWER KEY
Answers will vary. Encourage students to use their imaginations and accept all reasonable answers. For example, one answer could be that the student might have had problems completing a task that day, while another answer could be that the student was facing a difficult emotional situation and is struggling to find a solution.

G. Response Writing
○ Go over the directions.
○ Explain that this is a quick-writing activity and does not have to be perfect. Point out that response writing can be a warm-up to a more structured writing assignment, helping to generate ideas.
○ Set a time limit of 10 minutes.
○ Put students in pairs to read or talk about their writing.

Website Research
○ For additional information, refer students to these websites:
  • Freud Museum in London, England
    http://www.freud.org.uk/
  • Psychology Today Magazine: "How to Build a Dream"
    http://cms.psychologytoday.com/articles/pto-19951101-000037.html
  • Psychology Today Magazine: "Night Life"
    http://cms.psychologytoday.com/articles/pto-19980701-000025.html

PART ❹ THE MECHANICS OF WRITING, PAGES 157–160

○ Read through the introduction to Part 4 with students.

TOEFL® iBT Tip

TOEFL iBT Tip 4: Although the TOEFL iBT does not discretely test grammar skills, examinees' essay scores will be determined based on the range of grammar and vocabulary used in their essays.

○ Point out that the grammar activities in *The Mechanics of Writing* part of this chapter will help them improve their use of verb tenses as well as transition words for expository essay writing.

○ Recognizing these transition words and tenses will also help them identify information presented in a reading passage that is in an expository or narrative form.

TOEFL iBT essays may be scored higher based on whether or not the examinee can use transition words of time correctly in a sentence. Using verb tenses and more sophisticated phrases will help students improve their overall essay writing.

Using Transition Words of Time
○ Go over the information in the box about transition words of time.
○ Ask comprehension questions: *What are some adverbial conjunctions of time? When do we use a comma? What is chronological order? What are some subordinating conjunctions of time?*
○ Write two subordinating clauses on the board: *When I woke up from my dream, . . .* and *When I walked in the classroom door . . .* Ask for volunteers to finish the sentences orally.

A. Sentence Combining: Transition Words of Time
○ Go over the directions.
○ Have students combine the sentences using adverbial and subordinating conjunctions.
○ Have students compare sentences in pairs.
○ Go over the answers with the class.

ANSWER KEY
The order of clauses may vary.
1. Lucid dreamers know that they're dreaming while the dream is happening.
2. You need to replay the dream in your mind before you open your eyes.
3. He realized that it was only a dream as a dream enemy was chasing him.
4. Replay the dream in your mind; then open your eyes and write it down.
5. When Greeks were sick, they went to the temple of Asklepios.
6. First, you should focus on thoughts of flying during the day; second, you need to think about past flying dreams.

EXPANSION ACTIVITY: Describe a Process
○ Brainstorm a list of processes that students are familiar with (registering for classes, checking a book out of the library) and write them on the board.
○ Tell students to describe one process in at least five sentences. Remind them to use the adverbial and subordinating conjunctions.
○ Call on students to share their sentences with the class.

Using Verbs in Narration
○ Go over the information in the box.
○ Ask: *What tense do we usually use to tell a story? What are some other tenses that we can use? What is the narrative present?*

B. Using Verbs in Narration
○ Go over the directions.
○ Have students highlight the tenses in the paragraph in Activity B and in the description of the three dreams on page 156.
○ Have students discuss the tenses in pairs and identify the tenses used in each paragraph.
○ Call on students to read examples of different tenses in the paragraphs to the class.

ANSWER KEY
I go into my uncle's office. It's late at night, after hours. Nobody is there. I haven't come to take anything. I'm just curious. I look around and find it uninteresting. I'm moving from room to room. I notice that it's not a beautiful office at all, just functional. I notice with shock that there are video cameras hanging from the ceiling. There are several of them, and they're following me. I'm going from one room to another. I'm terrified and want to escape. I try to hide under a desk, but I know the cameras have already caught me.

ANSWER KEY, continued

Dream 1, page 156

I <u>was going</u> into a thick forest. There <u>were</u> so many trees that it <u>was</u> hard to see very far. I <u>decided</u> to climb a tree to try to see better. It <u>was</u> difficult to climb, and I <u>was going</u> really slowly. Finally, just as I <u>got</u> close to the top of the tree, I <u>slipped</u> and <u>fell</u> down, down, down. I <u>was</u> more scared than I <u>had</u> ever <u>been</u>. I <u>knew</u> I <u>was going</u> to die. Then I <u>woke</u> up.

Dream 2, page 156

I <u>was</u> at work. Someone <u>had found</u> a baby fox. I <u>was</u> amazed that this wild animal <u>was</u> here, in a city. It <u>was</u> a perfect creature but in miniature—just one-inch long. (I <u>didn't seem</u> to notice the impossibility of this.) There <u>were</u> three evil scientists who <u>were</u> excited about this animal. They <u>wanted</u> to raise it and then <u>do</u> terrible experiments on it some day. I <u>was</u> so angry, so furious, that I <u>couldn't express</u> myself. I <u>took</u> the baby fox and <u>ran</u> away. I <u>put</u> the animal in my purse to keep it safe. I <u>decided</u> to take it up into the mountains and let it go free where it <u>would be</u> safe. As I <u>was climbing</u> the mountain, my husband <u>joined</u> me. We <u>passed</u> farms and parks and lots of people. We <u>had</u> to find the wilderness. Finally, near the top, we <u>stopped</u> to rest at a university. When I <u>opened</u> my purse to check on the fox, he <u>wasn't</u> there. I absolutely <u>panicked</u>. He <u>couldn't</u> be gone! I <u>was</u> so careful! I <u>looked</u> everywhere, but he <u>was</u> gone. I <u>knew</u> I <u>would</u> never <u>find</u> him.

Dream 3, page 156

I <u>was</u> at a conference in Europe. It <u>had been</u> pleasant. One evening, we <u>were invited</u> to a dinner party at the home of a wealthy woman in Vienna. We <u>walked</u> into the home, which <u>was</u> incredibly beautiful. It <u>was</u> a combination of a castle, museum, and art gallery. There <u>was</u> rich, dark wood and Old Masters' paintings everywhere. I <u>had</u> never <u>seen</u> such art in a private home before. We <u>were</u> in a huge, elegant dining room, where waiters <u>served</u> many courses of fabulous food. There <u>was</u> so much to see. I <u>kept</u> turning around to watch the people and see the art. I <u>realized</u> that I <u>was missing</u> out on some of the food because others at my table <u>took</u> it while I <u>was marveling</u> at the art. But this <u>didn't bother</u> me because this experience <u>was</u> so special. I <u>was</u> completely happy.

CRITICAL THINKING STRATEGY: Analyzing Symbols

Analyzing symbols is an important critical thinking strategy. When creating written analysis of a work of art or literature (prose, poetry, drama, etc.) for an academic course, students will often be asked to analyze symbolism.

WRITING STRATEGY: Writing About Symbols

❍ Go over the information in the box.
❍ Ask questions: *What are symbols? What's an example of a symbol? What is light a symbol of? What is a circle associated with?*

C. Writing About Symbols

❍ Go over the directions and the example.
❍ Have students write sentences about the symbols.
❍ Have students compare their ideas in small groups.
❍ Call on students to share their ideas with the class.

ANSWER KEY

Answers will vary.

D. Talking About Symbols

❍ Go over the directions and the questions.
❍ Have students stand, walk around the room, and ask classmates questions about symbols.
❍ Have students write five sentences based on the chart, using the structures from the Writing Strategy box on page 159.
❍ Call on students to read their sentences to the class.

ANSWER KEY

Answers will vary.

EXPANSION ACTIVITY: Personal Symbols

○ Model the activity. Tell the class about some object you have that symbolizes something to you (*My car, a Miata convertible, symbolizes freedom to me. When my children were young, I drove a minivan, but after they went off to college, I wanted something more fun. I decided I needed a change, so I bought a sports car.*)
○ Give students a couple of minutes to think about something they have that is symbolic of their personality or place in life.
○ Have students write a brief description of the symbol and what it means. Tell students that the descriptions will be read to the class, and they should not include any names or identifying information.
○ Collect the descriptions.
○ Read a description to the class and elicit guesses as to the writer.
○ In a variation of this activity, ask students to draw or bring in their "symbols."

E. Review: Finding Errors

○ Go over the directions.
○ Have students find and correct the seven errors.
○ Go over the answers with the class. Have students explain what the errors are and how to correct them.

ANSWER KEY

In my dream, I was going into a thick forest. There were so many trees that it was hard to see very far. I decided to climb a tree to try to see better. It was difficult to climb, and I was going really slowly/; finally, just as I got close to the top of the tree, I ~~was slipping~~ slipped and fell down, down, down. I was more scared than I had ever been. I knew I was going to die; then I woke up.

I think this dream concerns my anxiety about beginning college. Freud would say that the forest is a "female symbol," and the tree is a "male symbol," but this doesn't make sense to me. According to the dream-for-survival theory, we dream about things that

concern us in everyday life. I've been worried about this big change in my life, so I think this theory is logical. The forest is probably symbolic of ~~I am~~ starting college. It was hard to see far into the forest, which represents my difficulty in imagining my future. Climbing the tree is associated with my attempt to control my own future. Falling is a symbol of ~~I am~~ being afraid of failure in college.

TOEFL® iBT Tip

TOEFL iBT Tip 5: Both the integrated and independent essays of the TOEFL iBT are scored based on how well the examinee completes the overall writing task. However, the writing section also requires that the essay follow the conventions of spelling, punctuation, and layout.

○ Point out that the *Finding Errors* activities in *The Mechanics of Writing* parts of each chapter will help students improve the grammar, usage, spelling, and overall flow of their essays.

EXPANSION ACTIVITY: Editing Practice

○ Photocopy and distribute the Black Line Master *Editing Practice* on page BLM 11.
○ Have students correct the paragraph and then compare ideas with a partner.
○ Go over the answers with the class.

ANSWER KEY

In my dream, I'm in a boat going down a river with my younger sister. The water is flowing very fast, and we ~~were~~ are afraid. I realize that there are more rocks up ahead and that the boat will turn over. We might drown. When I steer the boat near the shore, I make my little sister get out and swim. I keep

ANSWER KEY, continued

go~~ing~~ down the river. Water is often associated ~~of~~ ^with life. I think the river is a symbol ~~to~~ ^of life, and the rocks are symbolic ~~with~~ ^of the possible dangers we face. I have always protected my little sister, and in the dream, I realize we have to live our own lives. When she swims to the side of the river, that symbolizes ~~of~~ her own independence. When I continue down the river, I decide to face my own future, whatever it is.

PART **5** ACADEMIC WRITING, PAGES 161–163

Writing Assignment
○ Go over the writing assignment.
○ Have students read the names of Steps A–E on page 161–163.
○ Direct students' attention to Step A and have students choose a dream to write about. Encourage students to use one of their own dreams if possible.

WRITING STRATEGY: Gathering and Organizing Ideas
○ Go over the information in the box.
○ Ask: *How can you organize ideas for a narrative paragraph? What is chronological order?*
○ Direct students' attention to Step B. Go over the directions and the steps. Have students list the events in their dreams in chronological order and then create idea maps to analyze the dreams.

WRITING STRATEGY: Using Graphic Organizers: Idea Maps
○ Go over the information in the box. Read aloud Dream 2 on page 156 as students look at the idea map in the box.
○ Ask: *How does an idea map help you organize your ideas for a paragraph of analysis?*

Using Graphic Organizers: Idea Maps
○ Go over the directions and the steps.
○ Have students create idea maps to analyze their dreams. Remind students that an idea map shows relationships between events; it does not have to reflect the chronological order. Idea maps will vary in appearance, depending on the dream.

WRITING STRATEGY: Writing a Paragraph of Analysis
○ Go over the information in the box. You may want to read the example paragraph aloud as students follow silently in their books.
○ Ask comprehension questions: *What is one way to organize this paragraph? How can you make your paragraph more persuasive?*
○ Go over the point for students to notice in the example, and have them find the details in chronological order in the paragraph.
○ Read the *Analysis* directions. Ask students to high-light the expressions of symbolism. Have students list the writer's reasons.
○ Go over answers with the class.

ANSWER KEY

My dream about freeing the baby fox <u>is</u>, I think, <u>about</u> my desire to have a child because in the dream I felt protective and maternal toward the fox. The mountain <u>is symbolic of</u> my life, and the fact that my husband joined me <u>symbolizes</u> our marriage. Freud would say that the purse <u>is a "female symbol,"</u> and I think this is probably true. It's an "empty space," and I put the fox in it to keep it safe. The university <u>represents</u> education. To me, <u>it is associated with</u> my profession. I've worked for many years to reach this level in my work, and I haven't left much room in my life for a child. For this reason, it seems clear that "losing" the animal <u>means</u> that I know, unconsciously, that I won't have children.

Reasons for interpretation:
Desire to have children: feel protective and maternal
Purse as female symbol: empty space where she puts the fox to keep it safe.
Losing the animal: career hasn't left room for a child

TOEFL® iBT Tip

TOEFL iBT Tip 6: Both the integrated and independent essays of the TOEFL iBT are scored based on how well the examinee completes the overall writing task.

○ Point out that the *Writing a Paragraph of Analysis* activity will help students improve their coherence and the flow of ideas in their independent essays by taking smaller steps in their essay development.

○ Remind students that working at the paragraph level and demonstrating the ability to support their opinions more concisely will likely improve their overall essay scores.

Independent writing tasks may require that examinees analyze an idea, present an opinion or perception about a topic, or develop an argument about a controversial issue. Essay statements may be phrased in forms such as:

Do you agree or disagree with the following statement?

Some people believe X while other people believe Y. Which of these positions do you agree with?

○ Direct students' attention to Step C. Go over the directions and have students write their paragraphs.
○ Direct students' attention to Step D. Go over the questions. Have students read and edit their paragraphs, using the questions as a guide.
○ For peer editing, have students exchange paragraphs with a partner, edit, and return to the writer.
○ Go over the directions for Step E. Have students carefully rewrite their paragraphs and hand them in to you.
○ After you have read and returned students' paragraphs, you may want to set aside time for students to read each other's writing or display the paragraphs in the classroom. Have students keep all of their final versions in a notebook or folder so that they can see their progress and improvement over time.

●●●● PSYCHOLOGY

CHAPTER 6 ABNORMAL PSYCHOLOGY

In Part 1 of this chapter, students will read about culture and mental illness. In Part 2, they will read about behavior that may be considered abnormal. In Part 3, students will read about approaches to psychological therapy. Part 4 focuses on the mechanics of writing, including understanding and using the passive voice, a review of adjective clauses in definitions, writing about advantages and disadvantages, and using adverbial conjunctions of addition and contradiction. Finally, in Part 5, students will write a paragraph in which they summarize one approach to therapy and then present the advantages and disadvantages.

VOCABULARY

abnormal	depression	hydrophobia	motive	procedure
agoraphobia	disorder	illness	obsessed	psychoanalysis
alcoholism	dissociate	impending	outburst	psychological disorders
amnesia	distinguish	impulse	overcome	schizophrenia
anonymous	dizziness	insight	panic disorder	severe
anorexia nervosa	doom	intolerance	peak	systematic desensitization
behavior therapy	draw	irrational	perceptual	therapy
bipolar disorder	emotional	label	phobia	withdrawal
deceased	free association	likelihood	possessed	xenophobia
delusion	group therapy	major depression	preach	

READING STRATEGIES

Understanding Connotation
Finding an Implied Main Idea

CRITICAL THINKING STRATEGIES

Thinking Ahead (Parts 1 and 3)
Making Connections (Part 3)
**Using a T-Chart to Analyze Advantages and
  Disadvantages (Part 3)**
Analysis (Part 5)
Note: The strategy in bold is highlighted in the
  student book.

MECHANICS

Using the Passive Voice
Writing Definitions with Adjective Clauses
Writing About Advantages and Disadvantages
Using Adverbial Conjunctions

WRITING STRATEGIES

Paraphrasing and Citing Your Sources
Writing a Summary Paragraph

TEST-TAKING STRATEGY

Understanding Stems and Affixes

Chapter 6 Opener, page 165

○ Direct students' attention to the chapter title and picture on page 165.
○ Read the questions aloud.
○ Put students in pairs or small groups to discuss the questions.
○ Call on students to share their ideas with the class.
○ Ask: *Do you know who the artist was?* Give students some background information about Vincent van Gogh.

Culture Note

○ The painting in the chapter opener, "Hospital in Arles," is by the famous Dutch painter Vincent van Gogh (1853–1890). Dated April 1889, this painting shows the hospital in the small town of Arles in the French countryside. One of the most famous Impressionist painters, van Gogh produced more than 800 paintings and 700 drawings during his 10-year artistic career. His difficult life was marked by poverty and mental illness, but his genius and creativity is recognized around the world.

PART ❶ INTRODUCTION
CULTURE AND MENTAL ILLNESS, PAGES 166–170

EXPANSION ACTIVITY: Two Truths and a Lie

○ Model the activity. Tell students that everyone has something they do or some personality trait that other people might consider strange. Explain that you will tell them three things about yourself: two true things and one lie. For example, if you always sleep with a window open, always use a small nightlight, and always let your cat sleep in your bed, you could say, *I always sleep with a window open. I never let my cat sleep in my bed. I always use a*

small nightlight. Students must guess the lie. Note that in this game, you and the students will want to share only what they are comfortable talking about with the class.
○ Tell students two truths and a lie and elicit guesses about the lie.
○ Give students a couple of minutes to think of three strange things they can say about themselves (two true, one false). Remind students to put the statements in random order.
○ Put students in small groups to tell their two truths and a lie.
○ Call on students to tell the class something strange they learned about a classmate.

Before Reading
Thinking Ahead

○ Have students look at the pictures on page 166.
○ Go over the directions and questions.
○ Have students discuss the questions in small groups.
○ Call on students to share their ideas with the class.

ANSWER KEY
Answers will vary.

🎧 Reading

○ Have students look at the reading.
○ Go over the directions.
○ Have students read silently, or have students follow along silently as you play the audio program.

Culture Notes

○ About 3 percent of young American women suffer from an eating disorder. The mean age at which this disorder begins is 17.
○ Some researchers now believe that anorexia nervosa may not be entirely culturally bound. Cases have been found in very remote areas which are uninfluenced by Western culture.

Vocabulary Notes
○ Point out that much of the vocabulary in this reading makes use of affixes, or prefixes and suffixes. The use of affixes will be addressed explicitly in the test-taking strategy in Part 3.
○ You may want to have students highlight words with prefixes as they highlight new vocabulary.

Pronunciation Note
○ The addition of the suffix *–ical* shifts the stress to the syllable before the suffix. For example, the stress in psychology is on the syllable *–chol*, whereas in psychological it is on the syllable *–log–og*.

 EXPANSION ACTIVITY: Cultural Research Online
○ Write these two websites on the board:
  • Index of Culture-Bound Syndromes
    http://weber.ucsd.edu/~thall/cbs_cul.html
  • Stay Free Magazine: Curious Mental Illnesses Around the World
    http://www.stayfreemagazine.org/archives/21/mental_illness.html
○ Have students go to the websites and choose a cultural mental illness to research. Provide students with some questions to guide their research.
○ Have students share their findings in small groups.

After Reading

A. Finding the Main Idea
○ Go over the directions.
○ Have students highlight the sentence that contains the main idea of the reading and then compare answers with a partner.
○ Go over the answer with the class.
○ Have students tell what important words they highlighted as they read the passage and why.

ANSWER KEY
Students should highlight line 25: *However, what is regarded as a symptom of mental illness in one society may be just one aspect of a normal, healthy life in another.*

B. Vocabulary Check
○ Go over the directions.
○ Have students write the words on the lines.
○ Have students check their answers in pairs.
○ Go over the answers with the class.

ANSWER KEY
1. labels; 2. intolerance; 3. deceased; 4. obsessed; 5. possessed; 6. illness/disorder; 7. outburst; 8. amnesia

READING STRATEGY: Understanding Connotation
○ Go over the information in the box.
○ Ask questions: *What is a connotation? What is an example of a word with a negative connotation? A positive connotation?*

C. Understanding Connotation
○ Go over the directions.
○ Have students find three nouns that mean "psychological abnormality" that also have a clinical connotation.
○ Go over the answers with the class.

ANSWER KEY
mental illness, disorder, psychological disturbance

TOEFL® iBT Tip

TOEFL iBT Tip 1: The TOEFL iBT tests the ability to determine the meaning of words in context. Connotation versus denotation plays a large part in the way examinees will decipher meanings of vocabulary words used on the test.

○ Point out that the strategy *Understanding Connotation* will help students improve their vocabulary for the TOEFL iBT. By understanding the meanings of words and the emotions associated with those words, students will be able to apply this information toward further understanding the concepts presented in the text.

○ Remind students that the TOEFL iBT texts will often include glossaries of terms, low-frequency words, or specific phrases for which a dictionary might normally be necessary.

On the TOEFL iBT, this question appears in the following format:
   The word _____ in the passage is closest in meaning to . . .

D. Finding Important Details
○ Go over the directions.
○ Have students complete the chart with information from the reading and then compare ideas with a partner.
○ Call on students to share their answers with the class. You may want to copy the chart on the board and have volunteers complete different sections.

ANSWER KEY

Disorder	Symptoms	Culture/ Country	Influence of Culture
anorexia nervosa	inaccurate view of one's body obsessed with weight refuse to eat	Western cultures	Present in cultures where slender female bodies are desirable
dissociative identity (multiple personality)		Western cultures	seen as a disorder

ANSWER KEY, continued

amok	outbursts aggression amnesia	Malaysia and Indonesia	An expression of aggression in societies where such expressions are prohibited
possession by *jinn*	sickness	Algeria	A *marabout* must exorcise the evil spirits
brain frag	heaviness or heat in head depression anxiety	West Africa	
ataque de nervios	trembling crying screaming aggression	Latino cultures	

E. Synthesis
○ Go over the directions.
○ Put students in pairs to discuss the questions.
○ Call on students to share their ideas with the class.

ANSWER KEY
Answers may vary.
Amok and *ataque de nervios* both involve aggressive outbursts.

PART GENERAL INTEREST READING
What Is Abnormal?, PAGES 171–177

Before Reading
A. Thinking Ahead
○ Go over the directions and the questions.
○ Have students work in pairs to discuss the questions.
○ Call on students to share their ideas with the class.

ANSWER KEY
Answers will vary.

B. Vocabulary Preparation

❍ Go over the directions and the example.
❍ Have students match the definitions to the words.
❍ Go over the answers with the class.

EXPANSION ACTIVITY: Beanbag Toss

❍ Give students one minute to review the words and definitions from the vocabulary activities on page 169 and 172.
❍ Call on a student and toss a ball or beanbag and say one of the new words. Elicit the definition.
❍ Continue calling on students or have each student call on a classmate and toss the beanbag or ball.
❍ Continue until all the words have been defined.

🎧 Reading

❍ Go over the directions.
❍ Have students read silently, or have them follow along silently as you play the audio program.

Culture Notes

❍ The Ozark Mountains are in Arkansas and Missouri in the southern United States.
❍ Abraham Lincoln, the 16th president of the United States (1861–1865), governed during the Civil War. He was assassinated in 1865.
❍ Queen Victoria was queen of England from 1837 to 1901.
❍ Mark Twain is the pen name for Samuel Clemens, a famous American writer who lived between 1835 and 1910.

Vocabulary Note

❍ Both *psych* (spirit, mind) and *phob* (fear) are prefixes that come from Greek. Psyche was the lover of the Greek god Eros. *Phobos* means "fear" in Greek.

After Reading

A. Check Your Understanding

❍ Go over the directions.
❍ Put students in pairs to compare their answers and highlighted sentences.
❍ Go over the answers with the class.

EXPANSION ACTIVITY: Graphic Organizer for *What is Abnormal?*

❍ Photocopy and distribute the Black Line Master *Graphic Organizer for* What is Abnormal? on page BLM 12. Go over the directions with students.
❍ Have students fill in the graphic organizer with key words from the reading.
❍ Have students compare answers in pairs.
❍ Go over the answers with the class.

ANSWER KEY

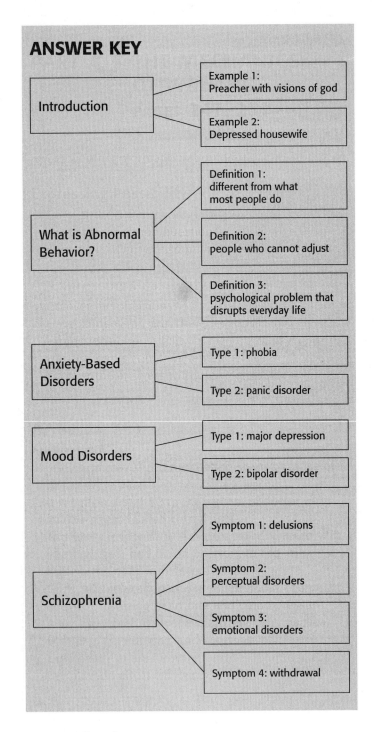

Introduction
- Example 1: Preacher with visions of god
- Example 2: Depressed housewife

What is Abnormal Behavior?
- Definition 1: different from what most people do
- Definition 2: people who cannot adjust
- Definition 3: psychological problem that disrupts everyday life

Anxiety-Based Disorders
- Type 1: phobia
- Type 2: panic disorder

Mood Disorders
- Type 1: major depression
- Type 2: bipolar disorder

Schizophrenia
- Symptom 1: delusions
- Symptom 2: perceptual disorders
- Symptom 3: emotional disorders
- Symptom 4: withdrawal

B. Application
○ Go over the directions.
○ Have students identify the problems and then check their answers in pairs.
○ Call on students to share their ideas with the class.

ANSWER KEY
1. depression; 2. schizophrenia; 3. bipolar disorder

C. Discussion
○ Go over the directions and the questions.
○ Have students discuss the questions in small groups. As an alternative, assign each group one of the questions to discuss.
○ Call on students to share their ideas with the class.

ANSWER KEY
Answers will vary.

TEST-TAKING STRATEGY: Understanding Stems and Affixes
○ Go over the information in the box.
○ Ask questions: *What is an example of an affix? What prefix means* against? *What stem means* marketplace?

Culture Note
○ The Agora was a marketplace in ancient Athens.

D. Understanding Stems and Affixes
○ Go over the directions.
○ Have students circle the letter of the best answer and then check their answers in pairs.
○ Go over the answers with the class.

ANSWER KEY
1. C; 2. D; 3. B; 4. D; 5. A

TOEFL iBT Tip 2: The TOEFL iBT tests the ability to determine the meaning of words in context.

○ Point out that the strategy *Understanding Stems and Affixes* will help students improve their vocabulary for the TOEFL iBT. Remind students that in the reading section of the test, scientific terms and academic vocabulary may be presented in the passage. These words usually have a Greek or Latin root.

○ Familiarity with prefixes, stems, and suffixes will help students make educated guesses about the meanings of words that they do not know. (Though this technique should be employed with discretion, students whose first languages are Romance-based can use this strategy if they are able to discern the meaning of an unfamiliar word in English by finding a true cognate in their native language).

PART ③ ACADEMIC READING
APPROACHES TO PSYCHOLOGICAL THERAPY, PAGES 178–187

Before Reading
A. Thinking Ahead
○ Go over the directions.
○ Have students discuss the questions in small groups.
○ Call on students to share their ideas with the class. Drawing on what students say, write useful vocabulary on the board.

ANSWER KEY
Answers will vary.

B. Vocabulary Preparation
○ Go over the directions.
○ Have students make guesses about the words and then check the definitions in the dictionary.
○ Call on students to tell the class how close their guess was to the dictionary definition.

ANSWER KEY
Student guesses will vary. Here are possible definitions: 1. urge/sudden desire; 2. reason; 3. get over/to succeed in controlling; 4. unreasonable; 5. process/ way to do something

CRITICAL THINKING STRATEGY: Making Associations
Making mental and visual associations between concepts is an important critical thinking strategy. In the following Expansion Activity, remind students that having a visual image of a word can help them remember its meaning better.

EXPANSION ACTIVITY: Draw Associations
○ Model the activity. Draw a picture on the board that illustrates or reminds you of one of the words in Activity B. For example, you might draw a computer on the board and the word *procedure,* because you remember the lengthy procedure you went through to fix a problem on your computer.
○ Have students think of associations for at least two of the words in Activity B and draw a picture for each.
○ Put students in pairs to explain their pictures.
○ Call on students to share their pictures with the class.

Reading
○ Go over the directions before the reading. Read the question aloud.
○ Have students read *Approaches to Psychological Therapy* silently, or play the audio program and have students follow along silently.
○ Elicit answers to the question from the class.

ANSWER KEY

Answers may vary, but here are the important points. The four types of therapy are:

1. Psychoanalysis—uses free association to make patient aware of unconscious impulses, desires, and feelings.
2. Behavior therapy—concentrates on what is wrong with patient's life and how to change it; sometimes uses systematic desensitization.
3. Group therapy—helps give person practical experience in getting along with others; family therapy is sometimes used.
4. Self-help groups—voluntary groups run without a therapist; members discuss a variety of problems; Alcoholics Anonymous is an example.

Culture Note

○ In the United States, a variety of mental health professionals can provide treatment for psychological disorders. A psychiatrist is a medical doctor who specializes in psychological disorders. A psychologist has a Ph.D in psychology. A social worker can also sometimes provide therapy and usually has an advanced degree or certificate in counseling.

Pronunciation Notes

○ This reading contains examples of the unstressed *that*. Examples may be found in the many clauses that begin with the conjunction *that* (*The idea behind behavior therapy is that a disturbed person is one who has learned to behave in the wrong way; The therapist might have the student make a list of all the aspects of talking to others that she finds frightening.*).
○ Note that when *that* is used as a conjunction it is unstressed. In contrast, when *that* is used as an adjective (*I hate that one.*) or a pronoun (*That is just gross.*), it is stressed.

EXPANSION ACTIVITY: Find the Unstressed *That*

○ Have students read the passage again and underline sentences that contain an unstressed *that*.
○ Put students in pairs to practice reading the sentences aloud.

After Reading

A. Check Your Understanding

○ Go over the directions.
○ Put students in pairs to compare the information that they highlighted.
○ Call on students to share their ideas with the class.

ANSWER KEY

Answers will vary.

READING STRATEGY: Finding an Implied Main Idea

○ Go over the information in the box.
○ Ask questions: *Are main ideas always stated clearly? What does it mean to infer? What is one way to infer a main idea?*

B. Finding an Implied Main Idea

○ Go over the directions.
○ Have students answer the questions and then compare answers with a partner.
○ Go over the answers with the class.

ANSWER KEY

Answers may vary.
1. antipsychotics and antidepressants
2. They are both medications to treat psychological problems.
3. Antipsychotics make schizophrenic patients less withdrawn, less confused, less irritable, and patients have fewer hallucinations. Antidepressants relieve depression.
4. Patients who cannot function within society, such as those with schizophrenia and severe depression, may be treated with medications (antipsychotics or antidepressants).

TOEFL® iBT Tip

TOEFL iBT Tip 3: The TOEFL iBT does not directly test the ability to determine the main idea in a text. Instead, examinees are required to recognize the minor, less important ideas that do not belong in a summary; or, they may be required to distinguish between major and minor points.

❍ The strategy for *Finding an Implied Main Idea* will help students distinguish between major and minor points in a text on the TOEFL iBT and link those ideas throughout the passage.

❍ This strategy will also help students use critical thinking skills to draw conclusions or make inferences based on what an author does not directly state in a text but implies. Questions on the test often require examinees to draw conclusions or form generalizations about what is implied in a passage.

C. Making Inferences
❍ Go over the directions and the questions.
❍ Have students answer the questions in pairs.
❍ Call on students to share their ideas with the class.

ANSWER KEY
Answers may vary.
1. The author thinks psychoanalysis is a time-consuming therapy that is not always effective.
2. Psychoanalysis might be the most expensive because it takes so much time and is one-on-one therapy. Group therapy, such as Alcoholics Anonymous, is probably the least expensive.

D. Making Connections
❍ Go over the directions.
❍ Have students write types of therapy on the lines and then compare ideas with a partner.
❍ Call on students to share their ideas with the class.

ANSWER KEY
a phobia: systematic desensitization
schizophrenia: drugs
alcoholism: group therapy
depression: drugs

E. Word Journal
❍ Go over the directions.
❍ Have students write their own sentences with the words they have put in their Word Journals.

CRITICAL THINKING STRATEGY: Using a T-Chart to Analyze Advantages and Disadvantages
❍ Go over the information in the box.
❍ Ask questions: *What kind of graphic organizer can help you analyze advantages and disadvantages? Why?*

F. Using a T-Chart to Analyze Advantages and Disadvantages
❍ Go over the directions.
❍ Have students complete the chart and compare charts in pairs.
❍ Call on students to share their ideas with the class.

ANSWER KEY
Answers may vary.

Psychoanalysis

Advantages	Disadvantages
one-on-one attention patient is "in charge" because he or she is doing the work complete examination	slow expensive psychoanalyst mostly listens all talk no action

Behavior Therapy

Advantages	Disadvantages
specific action-oriented uses relaxation	reasons not important

ANSWER KEY, continued
Group Therapy

Advantages	Disadvantages
experience getting along with others	less individual attention
sees others with similar problems	have to listen to others
sees how others see him or her	
helps a lot of people at once	
cheaper?	

TOEFL® iBT Tip

TOEFL iBT Tip 4: The TOEFL iBT tests the ability to read a passage, listen to a lecture related to that passage, and then write in response to a question based on the two stimuli. This integrated writing skill requires students to think critically about material that they have read, interpret that information, relate it to a lecture, and then present ideas in essay format. These reading and listening passages will often present a general principle and a counter example, or a problem and solution to which the examinee must formulate a response.

○ Point out that the strategy for *Analyzing Advantages and Disadvantages* will help students organize their ideas regarding two sides of an issue, and that they can use the T-chart as a tool when taking notes during the integrated skills section of the test.

EXPANSION ACTIVITY: Weigh Your Choices
○ Model the activity. Tell students about a decision you need to make (*what new car to buy, what to make for dinner, where to go on your next vacation*). Elicit options from the class (*Hawaii, Italy, Nepal*). Write the options on the board and then elicit advantages and disadvantages for each option.
○ Have students create and complete a graphic organizer for a decision they have to make.
○ Put students in pairs to share their ideas.

G. Discussion
○ Go over the directions.
○ Have students discuss the questions in small groups.
○ Call on students to share their ideas with the class.

ANSWER KEY
Answers will vary.

H. Response Writing
○ Go over the directions.
○ Explain that this is a quick-writing activity and does not have to be perfect. Point out that response writing can be a warm-up to a more structured writing assignment, helping to generate ideas.
○ Set a time limit of 10 minutes.
○ Put students in pairs to read or talk about their writing.

Website Research
○ For additional information on psychological disorders, you can direct students to the following website:
  • American Psychological Association Help Center http://www.apahelpcenter.org/articles/topic.php?id=6)

PART ④ THE MECHANICS OF WRITING, PAGES 183–187

○ Go over the introduction to Part 4.

TOEFL® iBT Tip

TOEFL iBT Tip 5: Although the TOEFL iBT does not discretely test grammar skills, examinees' essay scores will be determined based on the range of grammar and vocabulary used in their essays.

○ Point out that the grammar activities in *The Mechanics of Writing* part of this chapter will help them improve their abilities to write essays by using the passive voice as well as adjective clauses and adverbial conjunctions.

Using the Passive Voice

○ Go over the information in the box.
○ Ask comprehension questions: *Why do we use the passive voice? When do we leave out the* by *phrase? How is the passive voice formed?*

A. Using the Passive Voice

○ Go over the directions.
○ Have students rewrite the sentences using the passive voice.
○ Have students compare sentences in pairs.
○ Go over the answers with the class.

ANSWER KEY

1. Phobias are classified as simple phobias, social phobias, and agoraphobia.
2. Just four disorders are found in all cultures of the world.
3. According to traditional beliefs, that person was possessed by either demons or gods.
4. The specific symptoms of the disorder may be influenced by cultural factors.
5. Psychoanalysis has been criticized for being "all talk and no action."
6. Group therapy sessions are led by a trained therapist.
7. Self-help groups have been formed to deal with problems such as alcoholism.
8. "Amok," a behavior that is found in Malaysia, is characterized by a violent outburst.

Writing Definitions with Adjective Clauses

○ Go over the information in the box.
○ Ask questions: *What is an adjective clause? How can we use an adjective clause in a definition?*

B. Writing Definitions with Adjective Clauses

○ Go over the directions and the example.
○ Have students write definitions using adjective clauses beginning with *who* or *in which.*
○ Have students compare definitions in pairs.
○ Call on students to read their sentences to the class.

ANSWER KEY

1. Anorexia nervosa is a disorder in which people develop inaccurate views of their bodies.
2. A schizophrenic is a person who has lost contact with reality.
3. *Amok* is a disorder in which a person has a violent outburst.
4. A *marabout* is a traditional therapist who rids patients of evil spirits through exorcism.
5. A psychologist is a professional who treats people with psychological disorders
6. A panic disorder is a disorder in which the person has extreme anxiety.

Writing About Advantages and Disadvantages

○ Go over the information in the box.
○ Ask questions: *What structure can we use to talk about an advantage? How would you begin a sentence about a disadvantage?*

C. Writing About Advantages and Disadvantages

○ Go over the directions.
○ Have students choose two topics and then write three sentences about the advantages and/or disadvantages of each.
○ Have students read their sentences in pairs.
○ Call on students to share their ideas with the class.

ANSWER KEY
Answers will vary.

Using Adverbial Conjunctions
❍ Go over the information in the box.
❍ Ask questions: *Where do adverbial conjunctions often come in the sentence? What kind of punctuation do we use before and after adverbial conjunctions?*

D. Sentence Combining: Adverbial Conjunctions
❍ Go over the directions.
❍ Have students combine the sentences using *in addition, moreover, however,* or *on the other hand.*
❍ Have students compare their sentences in pairs.
❍ Go over the answers with the class.

ANSWER KEY
Answers may vary.
1. A person who hears voices of the deceased may be considered to be disturbed; however, in Native American Plains culture this isn't seen as a disturbance at all.
2. People who are agoraphobic usually stop going to movies or crowded stores; moreover, some will not leave their homes at all.
3. People with bipolar disorder suffer from deep depression; on the other hand, they also experience intense happiness and have great energy.
4. All of us are sometimes depressed, and there is nothing abnormal about this; however, in some people, the depression is intense and possibly dangerous.

E. Review: Finding Errors
❍ Go over the directions.
❍ Have students find and correct the errors.
❍ Go over the answers with the class. Have students explain what the errors are and how to correct them.

ANSWER KEY
According to Richard A. Kasschau in *Understanding Psychology,* psychotherapy $\wedge$^is^ based on the theories of Sigmund Freud. Freud believed that psychological problems are the result of conflicts in a person's unconscious. The psychoanalyst's task is to guide the patient through perhaps several years of sessions $\wedge$^in^ which the patient explores the unconscious motives for her behavior and becomes aware of the causes of her anxiety. One advantage ~~on~~ $\wedge$^of^ psychotherapy is that the patient can gain insight/$\wedge$;^however,^ a clear disadvantage is the lengthy process. Another implied drawback is $\wedge$^that^ the process takes so many years, so it is most certainly expensive.

EXPANSION ACTIVITY: Editing Practice
❍ Photocopy and distribute the Black Line Master *Editing Practice* on page BLM 13.
❍ Have students correct and rewrite the sentences. Then have students compare ideas with a partner.
❍ Go over the answers with the class.

ANSWER KEY
1. A disadvantage of drugs is that after leaving the hospital, patients might have problems with the real world. Soon, they might be back in the hospital.
2. A drawback of/to some of the antidepressant drugs is that they have side effects.
3. A therapist who practices behavior therapy sometimes has patients write a list of fears.
4. A principle of psychoanalysis is that patients can understand their own emotions; this understanding is called *insight.*
5. In Algeria, there is a disorder in which the person is possessed by evil spirits.
6. Self-help groups have been formed to deal with alcoholism, an addiction to alcohol.

PART ⑤ ACADEMIC WRITING, PAGES 188–191

Writing Assignment
○ Go over the writing assignment.
○ Have students read Steps A–E.
○ Direct students' attention to Step A and have students choose one of the three approaches to therapy.

WRITING STRATEGY: Paraphrasing and Citing Your Sources
○ Go over the information in the box.
○ Ask questions: *Why do we need to know how to paraphrase? What are some ways you can paraphrase effectively? What are some things that we shouldn't do when we paraphrase? When do you need to cite sources? What is plagiarism?*

Academic Note
○ One paraphrasing strategy that may help students who are more auditory learners is to have them orally restate or summarize information and record it. Then students can go back and listen to their oral restatements as an aid in their writing.

Paraphrasing and Citing Your Sources
○ Go over the directions for the activity.
○ Have students paraphrase the sentence and cite the source, and then compare paraphrasing in pairs.
○ Call on students to share their ideas with the class.

ANSWER KEY
Answers will vary.
1. According to Richard Kasschau in *Understanding Psychology*, drawing a line between normal and abnormal behavior can be difficult.

ANSWER KEY, continued
2. Kasschau points out in *Understanding Psychology* that abnormality may exist even though it is difficult to define.
3. Richard Kasschau, in *Understanding Psychology*, recommends caution when we judge a person to be "mentally ill" just because their behavior is hard to understand.
4. In *Understanding Psychology*, Richard Kasschau says that those who suffer from anxiety-based disorders cannot separate from their worries and fears and are full of anxiety.
5. Kasschau points out that some people's emotions prevent them from functioning in everyday life, and may even cause them to detach from reality, threatening their health or their lives.

WRITING STRATEGY: Writing a Summary Paragraph
○ Go over the information in the box.
○ Ask comprehension questions: *How does a summary differ from a paraphrase? Where in the summary should you cite your source? Can you write your opinion in the summary? What are some ways you can avoid copying phrases from the original?*
○ You may want to read the example paragraph aloud as students follow silently in their books.
○ Read the *Analysis* directions. Have students compare the summary to the paragraphs in the reading on page 173.
○ Put students in pairs to discuss the questions.
○ Go over answers with the class. Allow plenty of time for students to find and discuss the answers. The questions require close analysis and comparison.

ANSWER KEY
1. the article title, the author, and the topic
2. • The first definition in the summary (abnormal) is paraphrased from lines 18–19 in the reading: *any deviation from the average or the majority.*
   • The second definition (a person who cannot get along in everyday life) is paraphrased from lines 25–26: *abnormal people are the ones who cannot adjust.*

ANSWER KEY, continued

- The third definition is paraphrased from lines 33–34: *some ideal way for people to function psychologically, just as there is an ideal way for people to function physically.*
3. The summary uses simpler language. For example, the words deviation and adjust from the reading are not used in the summary. The summary is clearly stated in the writer's own words.

○ Go over the directions for the activity *Writing a Summary Paragraph.*

○ Have students summarize the paragraph on anorexia nervosa and compare summaries with a partner.

○ Call on students to read their summaries to the class.

ANSWER KEY

Answers will vary.
According to Pamela Hartmann in *Culture and Mental Illness,* anorexia nervosa occurs in cultures where the ideal female body is slender. In this relatively recent disorder, people are obsessed with their weight and often starve themselves because they have inaccurate impressions of their bodies.

TOEFL® iBT Tip

TOEFL iBT Tip 6: The TOEFL iBT tests the ability to read a passage, listen to a lecture related to that passage, and then write in response to a question based on the two stimuli. This integrated writing skill requires students to think critically about material that they have read, interpret that information and relate it to a lecture, then present ideas in essay format.

○ Remind students that paraphrasing is an important skill to develop. When listening to a lecture and taking notes, or reading a passage and taking notes, students must be able to then paraphrase and cite the information they wish to analyze.

○ In the integrated writing section of the test, students are encouraged to refer to information from the text or lecture. Excellent note taking and paraphrasing of spoken and written information will help students improve their overall writing skills for the test.

○ Direct students' attention to Step B. Go over the directions and the steps. Point out that students should write about the approach that they can describe the most clearly and have a lot to say about in terms of advantages and disadvantages. Have students write a short summary of the approach.

○ Direct students' attention to Step C. Go over the directions and the example paragraph. Have students write their paragraphs using the example as a model. Encourage students to choose a different approach so that they can generate their own ideas.

○ Direct students' attention to Step D. Go over the questions. Have students read and edit their paragraphs, using the questions as a guide.

○ For peer editing, have students exchange paragraphs with a partner edit the partner's paper, and then return it to the writer.

○ Go over the directions for Step E. Have students carefully rewrite their paragraphs and hand them in to you.

○ After you have read and returned students' paragraphs, you may want to set aside time for students to read each other's writing or display the paragraphs in the classroom. Have students keep all of their final versions in a notebook or folder so that they can see their progress and improvement over time.

EXPANSION ACTIVITY: Presentations

○ Have students research a famous person, past or present, who had or has a psychological problem (addiction, eating disorder, depression). Brainstorm a list of possible people before students start their research.

○ Instruct students to prepare a one-minute presentation on the person they researched.

○ Put students in small groups to give their presentations.

○ Have volunteers present to the class.

Unit 3 Vocabulary Workshop

Have students review vocabulary from Chapters 5 and 6.

A. Matching
○ Go over the directions.
○ Have students match definitions with words or phrases.

ANSWER KEY
1. h; 2. a; 3. e; 4. d; 5. f; 6. g; 7. c; 8. i; 9. j; 10. b

B. True or False
○ Go over the directions.
○ Have students fill in the bubble.

ANSWER KEY
1. F; 2. T; 3. T; 4. F; 5. T; 6. F; 7. T; 8. F

C. Words in Phrases: Prepositions
○ Go over the directions.
○ Have students write the prepositions on the lines.

ANSWER KEY
1. for; 2. with; 3. in; 4. at; 5. into; 6. of; 7. to; 8. of

D. Vocabulary Expansion
○ Go over the directions.
○ Have students complete the chart.

ANSWER KEY

	Verb	Noun	Adjective
1.	suffice	sufficiency	sufficient
2.	sacrifice	sacrifice	sacrificial
3.	tolerate	tolerance	tolerant
4.	obsess	obsession	obsessed
5.	envision	vision	visible
6.	signify	significance, sign	significant
7.	motivate	motive	motivated

E. The Academic Word List
○ Go over the directions.
○ Have students write the words on the lines.

ANSWER KEY
1. classic; 2. theories; 3. psychological; 4. conflicts;
5. aware; 6. motives; 7. insight; 8. procedure;
9. fundamental; 10. assists; 11. task; 12. relax;
13. method; 14. periods; 15. factor

UNIT 4 ●●●●● HEALTH

○ Direct students' attention to the picture on page 197. Ask questions: *What do you see? How is this picture related to the unit topic?*
○ Write *health* on the board and help students brainstorm words related to health. Ask: *What topics do you think will be in this unit?* Circle the words they suggest.

CHAPTER 7 MEDICINE AND DRUGS: ADDICTIVE SUBSTANCES

In Part 1 of this chapter, students will read about the consequences of addiction, especially on women and children. In Part 2, students will read about drug use and abuse worldwide. In Part 3, students will learn about addiction and what can be done about it. Part 4 focuses on the mechanics of writing, including a review of subordinating conjunctions, avoiding and repairing fragments, and the present unreal conditional. Finally, in Part 5, students will write a persuasive paragraph.

VOCABULARY

abstinence	cope with	given	prevalence	stabilize
addiction	crave	ingest	progressive	substantial
adolescent	culinary	inhalant	psychoactive	tolerance
adopt	cyclical	inject	psychological dependence	transmission
cannabis	death toll	intervention	relapse	withdrawal
chronic	detoxification	negligible	rely on	
codependent	disposable income	opium	seizure	
confidential	epidemic	phenomenon	sniff	
consume	fatal	physiological dependence	sober	

READING STRATEGIES

Understanding Metaphors
Noticing British English

CRITICAL THINKING STRATEGIES

Thinking Ahead (Parts 1, 2, and 3)
Making Predictions (Part 2)
Analysis (Part 5)
Predicting Opposing Arguments (Part 5)
Note: The strategy in bold is highlighted in the student book.

MECHANICS

Subordinating Conjunctions: Review/Extension
The Present Unreal Conditional
Identifying and Repairing Fragments

WRITING STRATEGIES

Writing a Good Proposition
Writing a Persuasive Paragraph

TEST-TAKING STRATEGY

Finding Sentences with Similar Meaning

CHAPTER 7 Medicine and Drugs: Addictive Substances

Chapter 7 Opener, page 199

○ Direct students' attention to the chapter title and photo. Read the questions aloud.
○ Put students in pairs or small groups to discuss the questions.
○ Call on students to share their ideas with the class.

PART 1 INTRODUCTION
CONSEQUENCES OF ADDICTION, PAGES 200–202

EXPANSION ACTIVITY: Vote with Your Feet

○ Write *Agree* on one side of the board and *Disagree* on the other.
○ Explain the activity. As you say a statement, students should move to the word that best expresses their opinion.
○ Have all students stand, or work with one group at a time.
○ Say a statement (*Drug abuse is a bigger problem than alcoholism*). Remind students to move to express their agreement or disagreement with the statement. Ask a few students to explain their position.
○ Continue with other statements and other groups of students as needed. Create your own statements or use the following:
   If people want to use drugs or alcohol, it's their own business.
   There should be strict laws regarding the use of all drugs, including alcohol and tobacco.
   People would be less likely to abuse drugs if the laws were less strict.
   Addiction is a big problem in all societies.

Before Reading
Thinking Ahead

○ Have students look at the photos on page 200. Ask: *What lasting consequences do you think the war in Afghanistan has had on women and children? How do you think opium production affects women and children? If a baby's mother uses alcohol or drugs during pregnancy, a baby may be born prematurely. What problems do premature babies face?*
○ Go over the directions and questions.
○ Have students discuss the questions in pairs.
○ Call on students to share their ideas with the class.

🎧 Reading

○ Have students look at the reading.
○ Go over the question.
○ Have students read silently, or have students follow along silently as you play the audio program.

Culture Notes

○ Kabul is the capital of Afghanistan. Thousands of people have died in Kabul as a result of the civil war in the 1990s and the continued fighting.
○ The Nejaf Centre is a drug rehabilitation center in Kabul.
○ Afghanistan is well-known for its hand-woven carpets that have been made in the country for hundreds of years.
○ Although opium was used in Greece since the 5th century B.C.E., it wasn't really produced in the Afghanistan-India-Persia region until 1500 A.D. Opium was exported to Europe and to China in the 17th century. For more information, direct students to this website:
   • BLTC: Opium
     http://opioids.com/opium/history/.

After Reading

A. Check Your Understanding
○ Go over the directions and the questions.
○ Have students answer the questions in pairs.
○ Go over the answers with the class.

ANSWER KEY
1. Babies are born addicted and children in the carpet trade are fed opium.
2. Symptoms include heart problems, hearing problems, vision problems, neurological impairments, deformation of the brain, and learning deficits.

READING STRATEGY: Understanding Metaphors
○ Go over the information in the box.
○ Ask: *What is a metaphor?*

B. Understanding Metaphors
○ Go over the directions.
○ Have students find the metaphor.
○ Go over the answer with the class.

ANSWER KEY
a messy room

TOEFL® iBT Tip

TOEFL iBT Tip 1: The TOEFL iBT tests the ability to determine the meaning of words in context.

○ Point out that the strategy *Understanding Metaphors* will help students improve their vocabulary for the TOEFL iBT. By understanding the meanings associated with those words and ideas, students will be able to apply this information toward better understanding the concepts presented in the text.

○ This skill will also help students with the rhetorical purpose question type, for which they will need to be able to determine why an author uses a particular way of writing or uses particular examples in the passage.

C. Extension
○ Go over the directions.
○ Have students discuss the question in small groups.
○ Call on students to share their ideas with the class.

ANSWER KEY
Answers will vary, but may include: health care costs; providing housing and care for babies whose mothers cannot care for them; special education in school.

PART GENERAL INTEREST READING
DRUG USE AND ABUSE WORLDWIDE, PAGES 203–211

Before Reading

A. Thinking Ahead
○ Go over the directions. Explain that *psychoactive* means "affecting mental ability."
○ Have students work in small groups to discuss the questions.
○ Call on students to share their ideas with the class.

ANSWER KEY
1. Other drugs could be cocaine, heroin, methamphetamine.
2. Drugs can be smoked (marijuana, crack cocaine, opium, hash, methamphetamine), injected (heroin), swallowed (pills), snorted up the nose (cocaine).
3. Answers will vary.
4. Abstinence is practiced in Muslim countries; in some cultures, women do not drink alcohol.

B. Vocabulary Preparation
- Go over the directions.
- Have students match the definitions to the words and then compare answers in pairs.
- Go over the answers with the class.

ANSWER KEY
1. c; 2. a; 3. d; 4. e; 5. b; 6. h; 7. g; 8. f; 9. i; 10. j

EXPANSION ACTIVITY: Original Sentences
- Have students write original sentences using any five of the ten new words.
- Put students in pairs to read their sentences.
- Call on students to read their sentences to the class.

C. Making Predictions
- Go over the directions and the questions.
- Have students discuss the questions in small groups.
- Call on students to share their ideas with the class.

ANSWER KEY
Predictions will vary.

Culture Notes
- The United Nations Office on Drugs and Crime was established in 1997 to assist countries in their struggle against illicit drug trade.
- The World Health Organization (WHO) is the health agency for the United Nations. It was established in 1948 to assist countries in helping their citizens achieve high levels of health.

🎧 Reading
- Go over the directions and the questions. Have students preview the reading by looking at the headings, captions, and box titles.
- Have students read silently or have them follow along silently as you play the audio program.

After Reading

A. Check Your Understanding
- Go over the directions.
- Have students work in small groups to check their predictions on page 204.
- Go over the answers with the class.

ANSWER KEY
Predictions may vary.
1. increasing; 2. Some diseases are transmitted by shared needles.; 3. alcohol, tobacco, marijuana, inhalants; 4. tobacco, alcohol

B. Vocabulary Check: Phrases
- Go over the directions.
- Have students answer the questions.
- Go over the answers with the class.

ANSWER KEY
1. disposable income; 2. death toll
3. Box 2: stabilization; Box 3: decline; Box 4: further increases

CRITICAL THINKING STRATEGY: Distinguishing Cause and Effect
Being able to distinguish between cause and effect is an important critical thinking strategy. Using a graphic organizer helps students visualize the relationships between cause and effect.

C. Finding Details: Cause and Effect
- Go over the directions.
- Have students complete the graphic organizer individually and then compare answers in small groups.
- Call on students to share their ideas with the class.

ANSWER KEY

Paragraph	Causes	Effects
Lines 9–29	growth of transportation, tourism, and communication	It is possible to transport drugs to distant places.
Lines 106–129	the use of heroin	Heroin is causing health and social problems.
Lines 130–146	changes in availability of drugs and location of countries	The practice of injecting heroin is spreading to many developing countries.
Lines 147–157	Glue is cheap, available, and provides a rapid high.	Glue is the substance which is most abused by street children.

D. Finding Details: Chronology

○ Go over the directions.
○ Have students complete the graphic organizer and then compare answers in small groups.
○ Call on students to share their ideas with the class.

ANSWER KEY

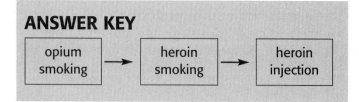

opium smoking → heroin smoking → heroin injection

TEST-TAKING STRATEGY: Finding Sentences with Similar Meaning

○ Go over the information in the box.
○ Ask: *Why do you need to know how to find sentences with similar meanings? What should you look for?*

TOEFL® iBT Tip

TOEFL iBT Tip 2: The TOEFL iBT requires examinees to paraphrase and cite information from written and spoken sources on the integrated writing skills essay. Reading sentences that have similar meaning can serve as models of paraphrasing in preparation for writing tasks.

○ Point out that the strategy *Finding Sentences with Similar Meaning* will help students locate information as well as identify a paraphrase of a sentence. Remind students that paraphrasing is an important skill to develop. When listening to a lecture or reading a passage and taking notes, students must be able to then paraphrase and cite the information they wish to analyze.

E. Finding Sentences with Similar Meaning

○ Go over the directions.
○ Have students highlight the sentences in the reading with a similar meaning.
○ Go over the answers with the class.

ANSWER KEY

1. Line 90: *The rate of decrease slowed throughout the 1990s, and by the turn of the century, cocaine use in the U.S. had stabilised at a roughly constant level. This stabilisation may demonstrate the cyclical nature of drug epidemics.*
2. Line 117: *The shared use of injection equipment has played a critical role in fuelling a number of local, national, and regional HIV-1 epidemics.*
3. Line 158: *Next to tobacco, alcohol is the most widely used and abused substance and is available in all but the most isolated areas of the world or in a few countries with strict religious prohibitions.*
4. Line 177: *Substantially fewer cigarettes are smoked per day per smoker in developing countries than in developed countries; however, the gap in per adult cigarette consumption is narrowing.*

EXPANSION ACTIVITY: Do It Yourself

○ Review paraphrasing with students.
○ Have each student paraphrase three sentences from the reading.
○ Put students in pairs to exchange sentences.
○ Have students find sentences in the reading that are similar in meaning to their partner's sentences.
○ Call on students to read their sentences to the class.

F. In Your Own Words: Summarizing

○ Go over the directions.
○ Have students complete the sentences and then compare ideas with a partner.
○ Call on students to share their ideas with the class.

ANSWER KEY

Answers may vary.
1. Paragraph lines 9–29 are about the global spread of drug abuse. The author says that social, economic, and political factors have contributed to this globalization of drug use.
2. Paragraph lines 106–129 are about heroin. The author says that heroin and the practice of sharing needles has a direct effect on the increase of health and social problems in many countries.

READING STRATEGY: Noticing British English

○ Go over the information in the box.
○ Ask questions: *What are examples of words that have different spellings in British and American English? What are examples of words that are singular in one but plural in the other?*

G. Noticing British English

○ Go over the directions.
○ Have students answer the questions.
○ Go over the answers with the class.

ANSWER KEY

1. amongst; 2. *Stabilized* and *stabilization* are spelled with an *s* instead of a *z*. 3. 1.1 thousand million, 1.1 billion

H. Discussion

○ Go over the directions.
○ Have students discuss the questions in small groups.
○ Call on students to share their ideas with the class.

ANSWER KEY

Answers will vary.

 EXPANSION ACTIVITY: Research on Alcohol/Drug Use by Country

○ Have students research use and abuse of a particular drug in their city, state, province, or country. Students can research independently or in small groups. Students can present the information in a paragraph or in an oral report.
○ Before students begin, brainstorm important information that they should look for (how many people use/abuse the drug, percentage of the population, problems that use causes, trends in use over time).
○ Discuss sources of information, such as the library and the Internet. For information about the U.S., students can go to this website:
National Institute on Drug Abuse,
www.drugabuse.gov/STRC/Forms.html
For information on world drug use, see the Global Youth Network of the UNODC:
www.unodc.org/youthnet/youthnet_youth_drugs.html.
○ Put students in small groups to share their information.
○ Call on students to tell the class what they learned.

PART ACADEMIC READING
ADDICTION: WHAT CAN BE DONE ABOUT IT?, PAGES 212–218

Before Reading

A. Thinking Ahead

○ Go over the directions.
○ Direct students' attention to the information in the box. Ask: *How many steps are there? What are some characteristics of the third step?*

○ In small groups, have students read the box and then discuss the questions on page 213.
○ Call on students to share their ideas with the class.

ANSWER KEY
Answers will vary.

EXPANSION ACTIVITY: Chart Another "Addiction"
○ Brainstorm with students a list of other "addictions" and write them on the board. Point out that some may be actual addictions (gambling) and others might just be time-consuming or problem-causing habits (Internet use, excessive TV viewing).
○ Put students in pairs or small groups to select an "addiction" and create a poster that shows escalating problems. Encourage students to use photos, icons, or other visuals on their charts.
○ Have students present their posters to the class.

B. Vocabulary Preparation
○ Go over the directions.
○ Have students write their guesses on the lines and then compare their answers with a partner.
○ Go over the answers with the class. If necessary, students should check their guesses in the dictionary.

ANSWER KEY
1. strongly desired; 2. handle, deal with; 3. not drunk; 4. depend on; 5. secret, private

---

EXPANSION ACTIVITY: Predict Content
○ Write the title *Addiction: What Can Be Done About It?* on the board.
○ Put students in pairs to answer the question in as many ways as possible. Set a time limit of two minutes.
○ Call on students to share their ideas with the class.

⌒ Reading
○ Go over the directions before the reading. Read the questions aloud.
○ Have students read *Addiction: What Can Be Done About It?* silently, or play the audio program and have students follow along silently.
○ Elicit answers to the questions from the class.

ANSWER KEY
An addiction is a physical or psychological dependence on a substance or activity.
Helpful: intervention
Not helpful: protect addict from consequences; help addict continue addiction

---

Culture Note
○ Alcoholics Anonymous was formed in 1935 when two alcoholics, Bill W. and Dr. Bob, met and decided that alcoholics could help each other quit drinking if they followed the 12-step program. There are over 2 million members in self-help groups around the world.

Pronunciation Notes: Prominence
○ Point out that in each thought group there will usually be one prominent, or stressed, word. Often when words are defined in the sentence, the word being defined will be stressed as well as a key word in the definition.
○ Demonstrate this with a sentence from the reading: *Tolerance means that the body becomes used to the effect of the drug.* Ask students to predict which words might receive greater stress or prominence (*tolerance, body, used to, effect*).

EXPANSION ACTIVITY: Prominence in Definitions

❍ Have students highlight or underline all the sentences in the reading that define or explain terms. (This will help students with the *After Reading* activities.)
❍ Have students mark the thought groups with slashes and then circle words they expect will be more prominent.
❍ Call on students to share their ideas with the class.
❍ You may want to replay the audio program to have students check their answers.

After Reading

A. Finding Details

❍ Go over the directions.
❍ Have students discuss the questions in small groups.
❍ Call on students to share their ideas with the class.

ANSWER KEY

1. Addiction is a physiological or psychological dependence on a substance or activity.
2. Codependents try to protect the addict from facing the consequences of the problem; they do not help the addict and can make things worse.
3. Family and friends can use a process called *intervention* to help the addict.
4. The two steps are to recognize that there is a problem and to make a decision to give up the drugs or alcohol.

EXPANSION ACTIVITY: Class Outline

❍ Photocopy the Black Line Master *Class Outline* on page BLM 14. Cut along the dotted lines and mix up the strips.
❍ Distribute slips of paper to students. Have students work together as a class to arrange the outline in correct order. As a variation, distribute a set of strips to small groups, and have each group arrange the strips in order.
❍ Have volunteers write the outline on the board.

ANSWER KEY

The correct order is shown on BLM page 14.

TOEFL® iBT Tip

TOEFL iBT Tip 3: The TOEFL iBT tests the ability to understand key facts and the important information contained within a text. Locating key facts and details in a text helps students improve their overall reading skills.

❍ Point out that the reading section of the TOEFL iBT requires examinees to identify information that is included in the passage.

❍ The *Finding Details* activity requires students to search for information in the passage based on *wh-* questions. This is excellent preparation for the factual information questions on the test and can later be applied to the classifying, categorizing, and organizing information questions.

B. Vocabulary Check

❍ Go over the directions.
❍ Have students write the correct words or phrases on the lines and then check their answers with a partner.
❍ Go over the answers with the class.

ANSWER KEY

1. physiological dependence; 2. tolerance; 3. withdrawal; 4. psychological dependence; 5. intervention; 6. detoxification; 7. relapse

C. Word Journal

❍ Go over the directions.
❍ Have students write words in their Word Journals.

D. Making Connections

❍ Direct students' attention to the poster. Ask questions: *What is this? What is its purpose? Do you think it is effective? Why or why not?*
❍ Go over the directions.

○ Have students work in small groups to develop a poster and a short radio commercial dealing with a specific problem and targeting a specific group.
○ Have students present their projects to the class. You may want to display the posters on the walls of the classroom so students can look closely at each.

EXPANSION ACTIVITY: Gallery Exhibit and Critique
○ Display the posters on the walls of the classroom.
○ Have students walk around the room to look at each poster.
○ Have students discuss what is effective in each poster.

E. Discussion
○ Go over the directions and the questions.
○ Have students discuss the questions in small groups.
○ Call on students to share their ideas with the class.

ANSWER KEY
Answers will vary.

F. Response Writing
○ Go over the directions.
○ Explain that this is a quick-writing activity and does not have to be perfect. Point out that response writing can be a warm-up to a more structured writing assignment, helping to generate ideas.
○ Set a time limit of 10 minutes.
○ Put students in pairs to read or talk about their writing.

🖥 Website Research
○ For additional information on substance abuse and recovery, refer students to these websites:
  • SAMSHA, U.S. Dept. of Health and Human Services
    http://csat.samhsa.gov/
  • Focus Adolescent Services
    http://www.focusas.com/SubstanceAbuse.html
  • Alcoholics Anonymous
    http://www.alcoholics-anonymous.org/
  • Prevline, U.S. Dept. of Health and Human Services
    http://www.health.org/

• Substance Abuse Treatment for Children and Adolescents
  http://www.aacap.org/publications/factsfam/subabuse.htm

PART ④ THE MECHANICS OF WRITING, PAGES 219–223

○ Go over the information about Part 4.

TOEFL® iBT Tip

TOEFL iBT Tip 4: Although the TOEFL iBT does not discretely test grammar skills, examinees' essay scores will be determined based on the range of grammar and vocabulary used in their essays.

○ Point out that the grammar activities in *The Mechanics of Writing* part of this chapter will help them improve the organization and coherence of their essays.

○ TOEFL iBT essays may be scored higher based on whether or not the examinee can use subordination in a sentence. Using conjunctions, connectors, and conditionals, as well as more sophisticated phrases, will help students improve their overall essay writing.

Understanding Subordinating Conjunctions: Review/Extension
○ Go over the information in the box.
○ Ask comprehension questions: *What are some conjunctions we use for cause? For condition? For contradiction? When do we use a comma before the conjunction?*

A. Understanding Subordinating Conjunctions
○ Go over the directions.
○ Have students work in pairs to discuss the different meanings of each pair of sentences.
○ Go over the answers with the class.

ANSWER KEY

1. Sentence **a** means the speaker was glad the drink didn't have alcohol. Sentence **b** means that the speaker liked the drink but might have liked it as much or more with alcohol.
2. Sentence **a** means that each time he has a drink, he feels sick. Sentence **b** means that the drink made him feel better.
3. Sentence **a** means when she found out she was pregnant, she stopped drinking. Sentence **b** means that she started to drink heavily when she found out she was pregnant.

B. Sentence Combining: Subordinating Conjunctions

❍ Go over the directions.
❍ Have students combine the sentences in two ways and then compare ideas in pairs. Remind students to make sure that both sentences have the same meaning.
❍ Call on students to read sentences to the class.

ANSWER KEY

Answers may vary.

1. a. We'll ask her to help us with this because she's both knowledgeable and dependable.
   b. Since she's both knowledgeable and dependable, we'll ask her to help us with this.
2. a. Although he knew a good deal about the danger of addiction, he began to use cocaine.
   b. He began to use cocaine even though he knew a good deal about the danger of addiction.
3. a. Her grades in college suddenly went down because she began taking drugs.
   b. As soon as she began taking drugs, her grades in college suddenly went down.
4. a. He adopted the baby even though he was informed that the birth mother was alcoholic.
   b. Before he was informed that the birth mother was alcoholic, he adopted the baby.
5. a. The baby's mother smoked crack cocaine before he was born.
   b. As soon as he was born, the baby's mother smoked crack cocaine.

Identifying and Repairing Fragments

❍ Go over the information in the box.
❍ Ask questions: *What is a fragment? What problem often causes fragments?*

C. Identifying and Repairing Fragments

❍ Go over the directions.
❍ Have students correct any fragments.
❍ Go over the answers with the class.

ANSWER KEY

1. Arthur was three days old when his aunt found him.
2. correct
3. He wouldn't let anyone closer than eight feet before he began hurling toys at them.
4. Street children in many countries use psychoactive substances such as glue or paint thinner.
5. correct
6. Indigenous people are those who were already living on their lands when settlers came from other countries.
7. In religious ceremonies, Native Americans traditionally used hallucinogens. For example, peyote and certain types of mushrooms helped them to have visions.
8. Because indigenous people used to have very strict laws and taboos about psychoactive substances, there wasn't such a problem in the past.
9. There wasn't much of a problem until indigenous people were exposed to "outside" attitudes and beliefs.
10. correct

The Present Unreal Conditional

❍ Go over the information in the box.
❍ Ask questions: *When do we use the present unreal conditional? How is the* if *clause formed? What form of the verb do we use in the main clause? When do we use a comma?*

D. The Present Unreal Conditional

❍ Go over the directions.
❍ Have students first identify the causes and effects and then write conditional sentences.
❍ Call on students to read their sentences to the class.

ANSWER KEY

The position of the clauses may vary.

1. (Magazine ads link alcohol with the idea of freedom and excitement,) so many teenagers are attracted to drinking.

    If magazine ads didn't link alcohol with the idea of freedom, many teenagers wouldn't be attracted to drinking.

2. Thousands of babies are born with serious physical and mental problems because (their mothers are addicted to crack cocaine.)

    If their mothers weren't addicted to crack cocaine, thousands of babies wouldn't be born with serious physical and mental problems.

3. Children sniff glue because (it is cheap.)
    Children wouldn't sniff glue if it weren't cheap.

4. (Street children don't trust adults,) so they don't go to centers for help.

    If street children trusted adults, they would go to centers for help.

5. There aren't taboos and laws to regulate the use of alcohol because (there isn't a tradition of alcohol use in the tribe.)
    There would be taboos and laws to regulate the use of alcohol if there were a tradition of alcohol use in the tribe.

6. (Hill tribes in Southeast Asia are now injecting opium instead of smoking it,) so there is an increase in the incidence of AIDS.
    There wouldn't be an increase in the incidence of AIDS if the hill tribes in Southeast Asia weren't injecting opium now instead of smoking it

7. It's especially important to establish treatment centers because (the number of addicts is growing.)
    If the number of addicts weren't growing, it would not be as important to establish treatment centers.

E. Review: Finding Errors
○ Go over the directions.
○ Have students find and correct the errors.
○ Go over the answers with the class. Have students explain what the errors are and how to correct them.

ANSWER KEY

The sale and use of illicit drugs should be legalized in the United States. First, the government cannot collect taxes on income that is made illegally, but if drugs were legalized, they ~~can~~ _could_ be taxed. This would be an enormous economic benefit to the country. For example, ~~marijuana in California.~~ _t_The largest cash crop grown in the state of California is marijuana, but the growers must now hide their profits/ _b_Because they are breaking the law. The taxes paid on legally grown marijuana, together with the money now spent on enforcing anti-drug laws, could be spent both on education to prevent children from trying drugs and on treatment for the thousands of addicts who want to be free of their addiction. Second, legalization would cause the price of these drugs to drop. As a result, many drug pushers ~~will~~ _would_ choose to go out of business because it wouldn't be profitable enough. Not only would some drugs be less available than they are today, but the crime rate in general ~~will~~ _would_ drop as crimes associated with drug trafficking ~~become~~ _became_ unnecessary.

EXPANSION ACTIVITY: Editing Practice
○ Photocopy and distribute the Black Line Master *Editing Practice* on page BLM 15.
○ Have students correct the paragraph and then compare ideas with a partner.
○ Go over the answers with the class. Answers may vary.

ANSWER KEY

Alcohol should not be advertised on television for several reasons. First, research suggests that children are affected by television advertising. For example, children are influenced by ads for sugary cereals. If children don't see so much alcohol advertised on television, they might not be influenced to try alcohol at a young age. Second, television commercials make the use of alcohol seem glamorous and attractive. If people didn't always see drinking alcohol as a positive activity, they would be more realistic about the problems of alcohol. Perhaps if commercials for alcohol were not so widely shown on television, people would be less likely to use it. Finally, the government needs to pass laws to limit advertising for alcohol. Of course, the television industry would lose a lot of money by limiting advertising for alcohol because beer companies are among the top advertisers on TV.

PART 5 ACADEMIC WRITING, PAGES 224–229

Writing Assignment
○ Go over the writing assignment.
○ Have students read the titles of the six steps, A–F.
○ Direct students' attention to Step A, and have students choose one question to answer in a paragraph.

WRITING STRATEGY: Writing a Good Proposition
○ Go over the information in the box.
○ Ask: *What do we call the topic sentence of a persuasive paragraph? What characteristics does a proposition have?*

Writing a Good Proposition
○ Go over the directions.
○ Have students decide if the propositions are good or bad, and if bad, state the reasons why. Put students in pairs to compare ideas, then call on students to share their ideas with the class.

ANSWER KEY
1. This is a bad proposition because it doesn't allow for other reasons of support and it is a matter of personal taste.
2. This is a bad proposition because it is a fact.
3. This is a good proposition.
4. This is a bad proposition because it is too broad.
5. This is a good proposition.
6. This is a good proposition.
7. This is a bad proposition because it is a fact.
8. This is a bad proposition because as written it sounds like personal taste.
9. This is a bad proposition because it deals with two points.
10. This is a bad proposition because it is a fact.

○ Direct students' attention to Step B. Go over the directions. Have students write a proposition and then read it to a partner for feedback. Remind students to use the characteristics of good propositions to evaluate each others' propositions. Walk around and provide help as needed.

CRITICAL THINKING STRATEGY: Predicting Opposing Arguments
○ Go over the information in the box.
○ Ask: *Why should you try to predict opposing arguments?*
○ Have students list at least two arguments that are in opposition to their own propositions.

TOEFL® iBT Tip

TOEFL iBT Tip 5: The TOEFL iBT tests the ability to read a passage, listen to a lecture related to that passage, and then write in response to a question based on the two stimuli. This integrated writing skill requires students to think critically about material that they have read, interpret that information, relate it to a lecture, and then present ideas in essay format.

○ Mention to students that the Critical Thinking Strategy, *Predicting Opposing Arguments,* will be useful in helping them interpret information from a reading and a listening passage. In the integrated task, students will be asked to compare and contrast points of view taken in a lecture or presented in the reading and draw information from each source to show that contrast.

○ Direct students' attention to Step C. Go over the directions and the steps. Have students work in small groups to discuss the questions on page 226.

○ Have students work individually to complete Steps 2 and 3 on page 227. Walk around to monitor this step and provide help as needed.

WRITING STRATEGY: Writing a Persuasive Paragraph

○ Go over the information in the box.

○ Ask comprehension questions: *How do you begin a persuasive paragraph? What is most important in a persuasive paragraph? What kind of evidence can you include?*

○ You may want to read the example paragraph aloud as students follow silently in their books.

○ Go over the points for students to notice in the example.

○ Read the *Analysis* directions. Ask students to answer the questions and create a graphic organizer depicting the causal chain.

○ Go over answers with the class.

ANSWER KEY

1. The example is about marijuana in California.
2. Both reasons are financial.

3. The present unreal conditional is used to talk about what would happen if drugs were legal, which they are not now.

4. Legalization ⟶ Drop in price
Drug dealers go out
of business ⟶ 1. Drugs less available
⟶ 2. Drop in general crime rate

5. The sources are articles by Smith and Choi.

TOEFL® iBT Tip

TOEFL iBT Tip 6: The independent writing task on the TOEFL iBT requires students to think critically about a topic and present their personal preferences or opinions in an organized format.

○ Remind students that the *Writing a Persuasive Paragraph* activity will help them when writing their argumentative essays. This strategy will also help students formalize their essays and scaffold the essay beyond the paragraph level.

○ The independent writing task often requires students to develop an argument about a controversial topic and use personal experience to substantiate their position on that topic.

○ Direct students' attention to Step D. Have students write their paragraphs. Remind them to use their notes in Step C and to address opposing arguments.

○ Direct students' attention to Step E. Go over the questions. Have students read and edit their paragraphs, using the questions as a guide.

○ For peer editing, have students exchange paragraphs with a partner, edit, and return to the writer.

○ Go over the directions for Step F. Have students carefully rewrite their paragraphs and hand them in to you.

○ After you have read and returned students' paragraphs, you may want to set aside time for students to read each others' writing or display the paragraphs in the classroom. Have students keep all of their final versions in a notebook or folder so that they can see their progress and improvement over time.

CHAPTER 8 THE MIND-BODY RELATIONSHIP

In Part 1 of this chapter, students will read about new medical research. In Part 2, students will read about the relationship between emotions and health, and how we can reduce stress-related illnesses through therapies that calm and relax us. In Part 3, students will explore another perspective on such treatments—the placebo effect. Part 4 focuses on the mechanics of writing, including expressing possibility, a review of conjunctions, and the use of italics and quotation marks. Finally, in Part 5, students will write a persuasive paragraph about the mind-body relationship.

VOCABULARY

alienation	defy	integrate	remedy
alternative therapy	device	likely	rife with
anxiety	dose	mug	sane
baffling	enhance	obesity	serenity
chemotherapy	fight-or-flight syndrome	outweigh	state of the art
chronic	gut	pace	stymie
clot	hostility	physician	sympathetic ear
combination therapy	hypertension	placebo	therapeutic
comparable	immune	psychosomatic	trigger
complementary medicine	impair	quack	wear down
conventional medicine	insight	rapid-fire	wound

READING STRATEGIES

Scanning for Specific Information
Guessing the Meaning from Context: Review of
   Dictionary Use

CRITICAL THINKING STRATEGIES

Making Predictions (Part 1)
Thinking Ahead (Parts 1, 2, and 3)
Seeing Two Sides of an Issue (Part 3)
Analysis (Part 5)
Note: The strategy in bold is highlighted in the student
   book.

MECHANICS

Expressing Possibility
Review of Conjunctions
Quotation Marks and Italics

WRITING STRATEGIES

Hedging
Writing a Persuasive Paragraph

TEST-TAKING STRATEGY

Determining Topic, Main Point, Purpose, and Tone

CHAPTER 8 The Mind-Body Relationship

Chapter 8 Opener, page 229
- ○ Direct students' attention to the chapter title and picture on page 229. Read the questions aloud.
- ○ Put students in pairs to discuss the questions.
- ○ Call on students to share their ideas with the class.

Vocabulary Note
- ○ The verb *affect* is commonly confused with the noun *effect*. *Affect* is almost always a verb and means "to do something that produces a change in someone or something." *Effect,* usually a noun, means "an outcome or result." Consult a dictionary for the use of *affect* as a noun and *effect* as a verb.

Culture Note
- ○ Yoga, a set of physical practices and postures to promote flexibility and health, originated in India. Yoga is very popular in the United States and classes are offered at most gyms and health clubs.

PART ① INTRODUCTION
WHAT DOES NEW RESEARCH TELL US?, PAGES 230–233

EXPANSION ACTIVITY: Category Sort
- ○ Explain the activity. Tell students that they will stand and you will ask a question. The students should walk around and ask their classmates the question, and then stand with people who have the same or similar answers to the question.
- ○ Ask: *How much sleep do you get each night?* Remind students to move around and talk to each other, so that they can group themselves according to response. When students are grouped, ask each group what answer they have in common.

- ○ Ask additional questions related to the topics in the chapter. Create your own or use the following:
  What's your favorite way to relax?
  What is the most nutritious food you eat every day?
  How many servings of fruit and vegetables do you have each day?
  How many hours of TV do you watch every day?
  What is your least healthy habit?
  What is your greatest source of stress?

Before Reading
Thinking Ahead
- ○ Have students look at the pictures on page 230. Ask: *How does this picture relate to the mind-body connection? For example, how does sleeping (the body) affect the mind? How does watching TV (the mind) affect the body?*
- ○ Go over the directions and questions.
- ○ Have students ask and answer questions with their classmates to complete the chart.
- ○ Call on students to tell the class what they found out.

ANSWER KEY
Answers will vary.

◠ Reading
- ○ Go over the directions and the questions.
- ○ Have students read silently, or have students follow along silently as you play the audio program.
- ○ Discuss questions and elicit answers.

ANSWER KEY
Research involving physical health: sunshine, hot cocoa, television
Research involving mental health: sleeping, sunshine, television, voting
Both: sunshine, television
Studies where stress plays a role: sunshine, voting

EXPANSION ACTIVITY: Personal Response

○ Remind students that one way to understand and remember new information better is to make personal connections with the text.

○ Model the activity. Tell students about a personal experience that you associate with one or more of the sections in the reading. For example: *One time in college, I was very worried about a final test. I stayed up all night to study. When I took the test the next day, I was so tired that I did very poorly on the test.*

○ Ask students to reread the passage and jot down notes next to each section that connects to their own personal experiences.

○ Put students in pairs to talk about their notes.

After Reading

A. Vocabulary Check

○ Go over the directions.

○ Have students write the words on the lines.

○ Put students in pairs to check their answers.

○ Go over the answers with the class.

ANSWER KEY

1. baffling; 2. insights; 3. triggering; 4. mug;
5. rapid-fire; 6. pace; 7. obesity; 8. likely

CRITICAL THINKING STRATEGY: Summarizing

Summarizing is an important critical thinking strategy. It requires students to analyze, classify, and reorganize what they have read.

B. Summarizing Research Findings

○ Go over the directions.

○ Have students complete the chart and then work in pairs to compare charts.

○ Go over the answers with the class.

○ Point out to students that this sort of graphic organizer is helpful when studying a textbook or when researching because it helps clarify key points.

ANSWER KEY

Topic	Where?	Finding (discovery)	Explanation
Sleeping	University of Luebeck, Germany	Sleep is good for problem solving.	Our brains continue to work while we sleep.
Sunshine	Montefiore University Hospital in Pittsburgh	Sunshine eases pain and improves mood.	Sunlight improves mood by triggering the release of "feel good" chemicals like serotonin.
Hot cocoa	Cornell University	Hot cocoa keeps you healthy and fights coughs.	The high level of antioxidants in cocoa helps fight cancer, heart disease, and aging.
Television	Children's Hospital and Regional Medical Center in Seattle	TV shortens children's attention spans. ; *TV watching linked to obesity and aggressiveness*	Rapid-fire pace may affect brain development.
Voting	University of Virginia	Voting improves mental health *because it helps you feel more in control of your life.*	Feeling more in control reduces stress.

TOEFL® iBT Tip

TOEFL iBT Tip 1: The TOEFL iBT writing section requires examinees to summarize major points and important details from sources. This is more evident in integrated tasks, but this skill can also be applied to independent writing tasks.

○ Point out to students that several activities in this chapter (vocabulary, scanning, main idea, details, and inference) will help them interpret what they hear and read and then write about the topic in their own words. Summarizing should be clear and succinct, without further explanation. The chart activity in *Summarizing Research Findings* will help students practice this type of skill.

○ Generally, students will have 20 minutes to plan and write a response to an integrated writing task.

On the TOEFL iBT, this question may appear in the following format:

Summarize the points made in the lecture you just heard, explaining how they compare to/ cast doubt on/refute points made in the reading. You may refer to the reading passage as you write.

C. Discussion
○ Go over the directions.
○ Have students discuss the questions in pairs.
○ Call on students to share their ideas with the class.

ANSWER KEY
1. Body: sunshine, hot cocoa, television
   Mind: sleeping, sunshine, television, voting
   Both: sunshine, television
2. sunshine and voting
3. Answers will vary.
4. Answers will vary.

PART ② GENERAL INTEREST READING
THE NEW SCIENCE OF MIND AND BODY, PAGES 233–240

Before Reading
A. Thinking Ahead
○ Direct students' attention to the pictures and read the questions aloud.
○ Have students discuss the questions in small groups.
○ Call on students to share their ideas with the class.

ANSWER KEY
Answers may vary.
1. Fear makes your heart beat faster and causes you to sweat and breathe faster. Answers will vary about how people react to fear.
2. Chronic causes of stress: noise, traffic, money, time pressures.
3. Other alternative therapies: yoga, deep breathing, biofeedback, homeopathic remedies
4.

Physiological	Emotional	Condition
	✓	alienation
	✓	anxiety
	✓	hostility
✓		hypertension
✓		obesity
	✓	optimism
	✓	serenity

5. Obesity can affect you emotionally. Anxiety, hostility, optimism, and serenity can all affect you physiologically.

Vocabulary Note
❍ The words *complementary* and *complimentary* are often confused because they are pronounced the same way. *Complementary* describes something that completes. *Complimentary* means "praiseworthy or flattering."

B. Vocabulary Preparation
❍ Go over the directions.
❍ Have students match the definitions with the words.
❍ Go over the answers with the class.

ANSWER KEY
1. f; 2. j; 3. b; 4. g; 5. a; 6. c; 7. e; 8. i; 9. d; 10. h

EXPANSION ACTIVITY: Beanbag Toss
❍ Give students one minute to review the words and definitions from Activity B.
❍ Call on a student and toss a ball or beanbag, saying one of the new words. Elicit the definition.
❍ Continue calling on students, or have each student call on a classmate and toss the ball or beanbag.
❍ Continue until all the words have been defined.

🎧 Reading
❍ Go over the directions and the questions.
❍ Have students read *The New Science of Mind and Body* silently, or have them follow along silently as you play the audio program.
❍ Elicit answers to the questions.

ANSWER KEY
The main way that the mind can affect physical health is through stress (or the control of stress). People can enhance their immune system through relaxation and meditation.

Academic Notes
❍ Point out that certain types of readings often use boxes to highlight information related to the main content of the reading. In journalism, such boxes are called *sidebars*.
❍ Point out the three boxes in this reading. Elicit ideas as to why this material is boxed.

After Reading
A. Check Your Understanding
❍ Go over the directions.
❍ Have students discuss the questions in small groups.
❍ Call on students to share their ideas with the class.

ANSWER KEY
1. Can we teach ourselves to be healthier?
2. Patients who have a good and trusting relationship with their physicians get better clinical results.
3. Ways to reduce stress: relaxation, talk therapy, music therapy, visualization, tai chi, prayer, meditation, paced respiration, repetitive activities.
4. Mind-body practices can help patients reduce stress; sleep better; cope with pain, anxiety, and depression; and enhance the immune system.
5. Mind-body practices help by lowering heart rate and blood pressure, and by reducing levels of stress hormones.

READING STRATEGY: Scanning for Specific Information
❍ Go over the information in the box.
❍ Ask: *What does it mean to scan? Why is it helpful? What steps should you follow when you scan?*

B. Scanning for Specific Information
❍ Go over the directions.
❍ Have students write the topics and phrases and then scan for the answers.
❍ Put students in pairs to check their answers.
❍ Call on students to share their ideas with the class.

ANSWER KEY

1. Topic: patient-doctor relationships; Phrase: *good and trusting relationship*; Answer: *These patients are more satisfied and so they get better clinical results.*
2. Topic: Stress and heart attacks; Phrase: *risk factor for heart attacks*; Answer: *The heart shifts into high gear and blood pressure rises.*

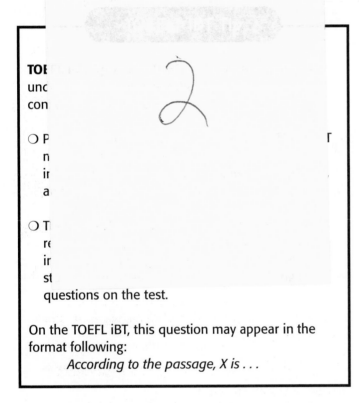

TO
unc
con

O P
n
ir
a

O T
re
ir
st
questions on the test.

On the TOEFL iBT, this question may appear in the format following:

According to the passage, X is . . .

EXPANSION ACTIVITY: Try It Yourself

O Have students write three questions that can be answered by scanning the reading.
O Put students in pairs to exchange and answer questions, following the steps in Activity B.
O Call on students to give examples of questions and answers.

EXPANSION ACTIVITY: Cause and Effect Chain

O Photocopy and distribute the Black Line Master *Cause and Effect Chain* on page BLM 16.
O Have students complete the graphic organizer by rereading the section "For a Happy Heart" on page 236–237 of *The New Science of Mind and Body*.
O Put students in pairs to compare answers.
O Call on students to share their ideas with the class.

ANSWER KEY

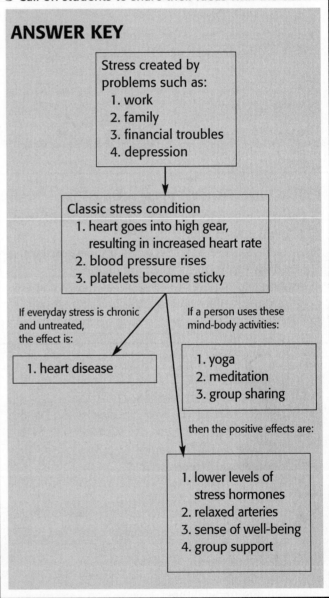

Stress created by problems such as:
1. work
2. family
3. financial troubles
4. depression

Classic stress condition
1. heart goes into high gear, resulting in increased heart rate
2. blood pressure rises
3. platelets become sticky

If everyday stress is chronic and untreated, the effect is:

1. heart disease

If a person uses these mind-body activities:

1. yoga
2. meditation
3. group sharing

then the positive effects are:

1. lower levels of stress hormones
2. relaxed arteries
3. sense of well-being
4. group support

C. Making Inferences

O Go over the directions.
O Have students jot down their ideas.
O Call on students to share their ideas with the class.

ANSWER KEY

T-cells are part of the immune system. (This is in support of the sentence *They also enhance immune function.*)

D. Vocabulary Check
○ Go over the directions.
○ Have students write the words on the lines and then check their answers with a partner.
○ Go over the answers with the class.

ANSWER KEY

1. gut; 2. physician; 3. dose; 4. clot; 5. wound; 6. combination therapy; 7. immune

E. In Your Own Words: Summarizing
○ Go over the directions.
○ Have students complete the sentences.
○ Call on students to share their ideas with the class.

ANSWER KEY

Answers may vary.
This article is about the mind-body connection.
The authors say that illnesses that are caused by stress can be reduced through relaxation therapies and better relationships between physicians and patients.

F. Discussion
○ Go over the directions and the questions.
○ Have students discuss the questions in small groups.
○ Call on students to share their ideas with the class.

ANSWER KEY

Answers will vary.

PART ③ ACADEMIC READING
A SKEPTICAL LOOK:
PLACEBO EFFECT,
PAGES 240–246

Before Reading
A. Thinking Ahead
○ Go over the directions and the question.
○ Have students discuss the question in small groups.
○ Call on students to share their ideas with the class.

ANSWER KEY

Answers may vary, but students will probably realize that if you think you should be getting better, you probably will.

READING STRATEGY: Guessing the Meaning from Context: Review of Dictionary Use
○ Go over the information in the box.
○ Ask questions: *When should you not use a dictionary? When is it a good idea to use a dictionary? Why is it a good idea to know or guess the part of speech?*

B. Guessing the Meaning from Context
○ Go over the directions.
○ Have students complete the charts and then compare charts with a partner.
○ Call on students to share their ideas with the class.

ANSWER KEY

Answers will vary.
Words that students may guess or look up include:
credit, ailments, incurable, palpitations, therapeutic, attributes, quack, double-blind, adverse, placebo, obscure, devices, rip-off.

EXPANSION ACTIVITY: Draw Associations

○ Model the activity. Draw a picture on the board that illustrates or reminds you of one of the words in Activity B.

○ Have students think of associations for at least two of the words in Activity B and draw a picture for each.

○ Put students in pairs to tell their stories.

○ Call on students to share their stories with the class.

🎧 Reading

○ Go over the directions before the reading. Read the question aloud.

○ Have students read silently, or play the audio program and have students follow along silently.

○ Elicit answers to the question from the class.

After Reading

A. Check Your Understanding

○ Go over the directions and the questions.

○ Put students in pairs to discuss the answers to the questions.

○ Call on students to share their ideas with the class.

ANSWER KEY

1. A placebo is something that has a beneficial effect, but the effect is not caused by pharmacological action or direct physical action.

2. The patient expects improvement and sometimes gets it. The placebo may relive tension and anxiety.

3. A "nocebo" is something that produces negative effects, although there is not pharmacological or direct physical action.

4. Placebos: sugar pills, heat, light, hydrotherapy, manipulation, massage, various gadgets, vitamins, tonics

TEST-TAKING STRATEGY: Determining Topic, Main Point, Purpose, and Tone

○ Go over the information in the box.

○ Ask questions: *How can you determine the purpose of a reading? How can you find the tone?*

B. Determining Topic, Main Point, Purpose, and Tone

○ Go over the directions.

○ Have students circle the answers and then compare answers with a partner.

○ Go over the answers with the class.

ANSWER KEY

1. A; 2. C; 3. D; 4. A

TOEFL® iBT Tip

TOEFL iBT Tip 3: The TOEFL iBT does not directly test the ability to determine the main idea in a text. Instead, examinees are required to recognize the minor, less important ideas that do not belong in a summary; or, they may be required to distinguish between major and minor points of information.

○ Point out that the strategy for *Determining Topic, Main Point, Purpose, and Tone* will help students distinguish between major and minor points in a text on the TOEFL iBT. Classifying, categorizing, and organizing information questions, and rhetorical purpose type questions will require these overall basic comprehension strategies.

C. Vocabulary Check

○ Go over the directions.

○ Have students write the words or phrases on the lines and then check their answers in pairs.

○ Go over the answers with the class.

ANSWER KEY

1. psychosomatic; 2. symptoms; 3. devices; 4. quacks

D. Word Journal

○ Go over the directions.

○ Have students write words in their Word Journals.

CRITICAL THINKING STRATEGY: Seeing Two Sides of an Issue

❍ Go over the information in the box.
❍ Ask: *Why do you need to see both sides of an issue?*

E. Seeing Two Sides of an Issue

❍ Go over the directions and the steps.
❍ Put students into an even number of small groups. Assign half the groups to find evidence to support the mind-body activities, and tell half to find evidence critical of these activities.
❍ Match each group with an opposing group so that each group supporting mind-body activities is joined with a group critical of mind-body activities.
❍ Go over the ways to express disagreement politely.
❍ Have the groups discuss the activities and exchange evidence.

ANSWER KEY

Answers may vary.

TOEFL® iBT Tip

TOEFL iBT Tip 4: The integrated writing skill on the TOEFL iBT requires students to think critically about material that they have read, interpret that information, relate it to a lecture, and then present ideas in essay format.

❍ Point out that the *Seeing Two Sides of an Issue* activity corresponds to a strategy they will need to use when writing both integrated and independent essays.

❍ They may be presented with two ideas and asked to argue for or against one of those ideas or state a personal preference about an issue. They may also be required to listen to part of a lecture or conversation and read a related text, and then analyze both sides of an issue.

EXPANSION ACTIVITY: Debate

❍ Tell students that they are going to debate the issues related to mind-body activities.
❍ Explain the format. Two opposing groups will debate. One member of each group will serve as the judges. The other members will take turns presenting the arguments to support their positions. You may want to set a time limit of two minutes for each side, with one minute of rebuttal. The two judges for each debate will decide which side wins according to the strength of the evidence.
❍ Have the groups debate. Walk around to monitor the activity.
❍ Call on student judges to tell the class about the debate they observed.

F. Discussion

❍ Go over the directions and the quotations in the box.
❍ Have students discuss the questions in small groups.
❍ Call on students to share their ideas with the class.

ANSWER KEY

Answers will vary.

G. Response Writing

❍ Go over the directions.
❍ Explain that this is a quick-writing activity and does not have to be perfect.
❍ Set a time limit of 10 minutes.
❍ Put students in pairs to read or talk about their writing.

Website Research

❍ For additional information on mind-body medicine, refer students to these websites:
  • Mind Body Medical Institute
    http://www.mbmi.org/default.asp
  • Alternative Medicine Foundation
    http://www.amfoundation.org/mindbodymed.htm
  • American Board of Family Practice
    http://www.jabfp.org/cgi/content/full/16/2/131
  • Advances in Mind-Body Medicine
    http://www.advancesjournal.com/aj/login/index.jsp

PART ④ THE MECHANICS OF WRITING, PAGES 247–251

○ Go over the information about Part 4.

Expressing Possibility
○ Go over the information in the box.
○ Ask comprehension questions: *How can we express possibility? What are some modals of possibility?*

A. Expressing Possibility
○ Go over the directions.
○ Have students answer the questions using expressions of possibility.
○ Have students compare sentences in pairs.
○ Go over the answers with the class.

ANSWER KEY
Answers may vary.
1. Television may shorten attention spans because of its rapid-fire pace.
2. It is believed that 60 to 90 percent of doctor visits involve stress-related complaints.
3. The stress response, which causes the heart to shift into high gear and blood pressure to rise, may explain the danger of severe stress.
4. Conscious relaxation and meditation can counteract stress by lowering heart rate and blood pressure.
5. A lactose tablet may relieve anxiety, pain, nausea, vomiting, palpitations, and shortness of breath.
6. Confidence in the treatment makes it more likely the placebo effect will occur.

Review of Conjunctions
○ Go over the information in the box.
○ Ask questions: *What is a coordinating conjunction we can use for contradiction? What is a subordinating conjunction we can use for cause and effect? What kind of conjunction is* thus?

B. Sentence Combining: Conjunctions
○ Go over the directions.
○ Have students combine each pair of sentences using the indicated types of conjunctions.
○ Have students compare sentences in pairs.
○ Call on students to read their sentences to the class.

ANSWER KEY
Answers may vary.
1. Cocoa is more healthful than tea for it has more antioxidants, which fight cancer, heart disease, and aging.
   Cocoa is more healthful than tea because it has more antioxidants, which fight cancer, heart disease, and aging.
   Cocoa has more antioxidants, which fight cancer, heart disease, and aging; as a result, it is more healthful than tea.
2. Stress isn't as bad for the health as smoking, but it is as bad as high blood pressure.
   Stress isn't as bad for the health as smoking, although it is as bad as high blood pressure.
   Stress isn't as bad for the health as smoking; however, it is as bad as high blood pressure.
3. Many symptoms have a psychological component, so treatment that lessens tension can help reduce the symptoms.
   Since many symptoms have a psychological component, treatment that lessens tension can help reduce the symptoms.
   Many symptoms have a psychological component; consequently, treatment that lessens tension can help reduce the symptoms.
4. Ten to twenty minutes of meditation is ideal, but even five minutes can leave you calm.
   While ten to twenty minutes of meditation is ideal, even five minutes can leave you calm.
   Ten to twenty minutes of meditation is ideal; nevertheless, even five minutes can leave you calm.
5. Placebo responses can be dangerous for they can obscure real disease and lead to delay in treatment.
   Placebo responses can be dangerous because they can obscure real disease and lead to delay in treatment.
   Placebo responses can be dangerous; as a result, they can obscure real disease and lead to delay in treatment.

Using Italics and Quotation Marks
○ Go over the information in the box.
○ Ask questions: *How do we write the title of a movie? What punctuation do we use for the title of a short story? What do we use for emphasis? What do we use to indicate the word has a different meaning from its usual meaning?*
○ Remind students that when handwriting, they can underline to indicate italics.

C. Using Italics and Quotation Marks
○ Go over the directions.
○ Have students write the reasons on the lines.
○ Go over the answers with the class.

ANSWER KEY
1. for the meaning of the word; 2. different or opposite use; 3. emphasis; 4. direct quote; 5. title of a book; 6. to mean "the word . . ."; 7. for the meaning of the word; 8. foreign word

EXPANSION ACTIVITY: Find Examples
○ Bring in examples of readings from textbooks, magazine articles, online articles, and newspapers, or have students bring in examples as an out-of-class assignment.
○ Have students find as many examples as they can of different uses of italics and quotation marks.
○ Put students in pairs to compare ideas.
○ Call on students to share examples with the class.

Using Quotation Marks
○ Go over the information in the box.
○ Ask questions: *What is an attribution? Where can you put an attribution when quoting material?*

D. Review: Finding Errors
○ Go over the directions.
○ Have students find and correct the six errors.
○ Go over the answers with the class. Call on students to explain what the errors are and how to correct them.

ANSWER KEY
Many people are skeptical about attempts to improve health through mind-body medicine. Stephen Barrett, for example, is critical of doctors "who rely on the placebo effect" and calls them " quacks." However, mind-body relaxation techniques can be an effective way to reduce stress, which is a serious risk factor for heart disease. In a 2004 study, it was found that stress is "comparable to risk factors like hypertension and abdominal obesity," according to Dr. Salim Yusuf of McMaster University. The problem seems to be chronic stress. Although it may be not possible to escape long-term stressful situations in life, relaxation exercises such as yoga are beneficial to cardiac health. In Newsweek, Anne Underwood explains that this happens by "lowering levels of stress hormones and helping to relax arteries." Relaxation might be just a placebo; nevertheless, even Barrett admits that placebos reduce a patient's anxiety and thereby "may relieve symptoms caused by the body's reaction to tension." When it comes to the prevention of heart attacks, this is a benefit.

TOEFL® iBT Tip

TOEFL iBT Tip 5: Both the integrated and independent essays of the TOEFL iBT are scored based on how well the examinee completes the overall writing task. However, the writing section also requires that the essay follow the conventions of spelling, punctuation, and layout.

○ Point out that the *Finding Errors* activity in *The Mechanics of Writing* part of this chapter will help students improve their grammar, usage, spelling, and the overall flow of their essays.

EXPANSION ACTIVITY: Editing Practice

○ Photocopy and distribute the Black Line Master *Editing Practice* on page BLM 17.
○ Have students correct the paragraph and then compare ideas with a partner.
○ Go over the answers with the class.

ANSWER KEY

According to Lynn Payer ∧ the author of <u>Medicine and Culture</u> ∧ European medicine is quite different from American medicine/; for example, doctors in England are rather conservative. English doctors don't often give physical exams or prescribe drugs frequently/ ₿ᵇecause they believe that no treatment is better than incorrect and unnecessary treatment. While physicians in the United States focus on bacteria and other external causes of disease∕∧ French doctors believe that a patient's general physical condition is equally important. For this reason ∧ French doctors prescribe vitamins more often than antibiotics.

PART ⑤ ACADEMIC WRITING
PAGES 252–256

Writing Assignment

○ Go over the writing assignment.
○ Have students read the titles of the six steps, A–F.
○ Direct students' attention to Step A, and have students choose one of the topics (A, B, C, or D). Point out that if students choose topics A or B, they will just choose one of the listed possibilities.

WRITING STRATEGY: Hedging

○ Go over the information in the box.
○ Ask: *Why do we need to hedge in academic writing? What words should we stay away from? What are some adverbs that help us hedge? What are some verbs that can be used to hedge?*

Hedging

○ Go over the directions for the activity.
○ Have students circle the letter of the sentence that uses hedging and then check their answers in pairs. Go over the answers with the class.

ANSWER KEY

1. B; 2. A; 3. B; 4. B; 5. A

TOEFL® iBT Tip

TOEFL iBT Tip 6: Both the integrated and independent essays of the TOEFL iBT are scored based on how well the examinee completes the overall writing task.

○ Point out that *Hedging* can be a useful strategy to use in the writing section when you want to avoid expressing an opinion that you cannot prove.

○ In the integrated essay section, examinees will have to make generalizations or form their own opinions about information that they have read and heard. The ability to use hedging strategies will help improve their overall writing skills.

EXPANSION ACTIVITY: HEDGE IT

○ Model the activity. Write a sentence on the board that does not use hedging (*Mind-body practices will improve the health of everyone who tries them*). Elicit ways that the sentence can be rewritten to soften the message (*Mind-body practices may improve the health of the people who try them; Mind-body practices will often improve the health . . .; Mind-body practices will improve the health of many of the people . . .*).
○ Have students write five statements about mind-body activities that don't use hedges.
○ Put students in pairs to exchange and rewrite the sentences using hedges.
○ Call on students to read their sentences to the class.

○ Direct students' attention to Step B. Have students write their propositions. You may want to have students share their propositions in pairs to receive feedback. Remind students to look back at page 224 for help in evaluating propositions.

○ Direct students' attention to Step C. Go over the directions. Have students write the evidence for their propositions and note the sources.

WRITING STRATEGY: Writing a Persuasive Paragraph

○ Go over the information in the box.
○ Ask comprehension questions: *Where do we usually write a topic sentence? What is different about many persuasive paragraphs? Why do you think this is so?*
○ You may want to read the example paragraph aloud as students follow silently in their books.
○ Go over the points for students to notice in the example.
○ Read the *Analysis* directions. Ask students to answer the questions and highlight the adverbial conjunctions, subordinating conjunctions, and quoted information.
○ Go over answers with the class.

ANSWER KEY

1. However, mind-body relaxation techniques can be an effective way to reduce stress, which is a serious risk factor for heart disease.
2. can be
3. relaxation techniques
4. They state the opposing argument.
5 and 6: See underlining below.
7. *can be, seems to be, may not be possible, might be, may relieve*

Many people are skeptical about attempts to improve health through mind-body medicine. Stephen Barrett, for example, is critical of doctors "who rely on the placebo effect" and calls them "quacks." However, mind-body relaxation techniques can be an effective way to reduce stress, which is a serious risk factor for heart disease. In a 2004 study, it was found that stress is "comparable to risk factors like hypertension and abdominal obesity," according

to Dr. Salim Yusuf of McMaster University. The problem seems to be chronic stress. Although it may not be possible to escape long-term stressful situations in life, relaxation exercises such as yoga are beneficial to cardiac health. In *Newsweek*, Anne Underwood explains that this happens by "lowering levels of stress hormones and helping to relax arteries." Relaxation might be just a placebo. Nevertheless, even Barrett admits that placebos reduce a patient's anxiety and thereby "may relieve symptoms caused by the body's reaction to tension." When it comes to the prevention of heart attacks, this is a benefit.

○ Direct students' attention to Step D. Have them write their paragraphs, beginning with the opposing argument. Provide help as needed.
○ Direct students' attention to Step E. Go over the questions. Have students read and edit their paragraphs, using the questions as a guide.
○ For peer editing, have students exchange paragraphs with a partner, edit, and return to the writer.
○ Go over the directions for Step F. Have students carefully rewrite their paragraphs and hand them in to you.
○ After you have read and returned students' paragraphs, you may want to set aside time for students to read each other's writing or display the paragraphs in the classroom. Have students keep all of their final versions in a notebook or folder so that they can see their progress and improvement over time.

EXPANSION ACTIVITY: Presentations

○ Have students research a topic related to the content of the chapter such as a specific mind-body practice or a specific research experiment on mind-body activities.
○ Instruct students to prepare a one-minute presentation on the topic they researched.
○ Put students in small groups to give their presentations.
○ Ask for volunteers to present to the class.

Unit 4 Vocabulary Workshop

Have students review vocabulary from Chapters 7 and 8.

A. Matching
○ Go over the directions.
○ Have students match definitions with words or phrases.

ANSWER KEY
1. h; 2. i; 3. a; 4. d; 5. c; 6. f; 7. b; 8. e; 9. g; 10. j

B. Vocabulary Expansion
○ Go over the directions.
○ Tell students to complete the chart.

ANSWER KEY

	Verb	Noun	Adjective
1.	withdraw	withdrawal	withdrawn
2.	alienate	alienation	alienated
3.	consume	consumer, consumption	consumable
4.	compare	comparison	comparable
5.	ail	ailment	ailing
6.	impair	impairment	impaired
7.	sober	sobriety	sober
8.	defy	defiance	defiant

C. Words in Phrases
○ Go over the directions.
○ Have students write the words on the lines.

ANSWER KEY
1. span; 2. pace; 3. art; 4–6. inhale, inject, smoke; 7. with; 8. on; 9. down; 10. with

D. The Academic Word List
○ Go over the directions.
○ Have students write the words on the lines.

ANSWER KEY
1. affect; 2. physical; 3. source; 4. potential; 5. stress; 6. percent; 7. involve; 8. researchers; 9. credit; 10. sufficient; 11. variation; 12. temporary; 13. misinterpret; 14. evidence; 15. establish

APPENDIX 1 COMMON IRREGULAR VERBS

Simple Present	Simple Past	Past Participle	Simple Present	Simple Past	Past Participle
am/is/are	was/were	been	mean	meant	meant
beat	beat	beat	meet	met	met
become	became	become	pay	paid	paid
begin	began	begun	put	put	put
break	broke	broken	read	read	read
bring	brought	brought	ride	rode	ridden
buy	bought	bought	ring	rang	rung
catch	caught	caught	rise	rose	risen
choose	chose	chosen	run	ran	run
come	come	come	say	said	said
cost	cost	cost	see	saw	seen
cut	cut	cut	send	sent	sent
do	done	done	set	set	set
draw	drew	drawn	shake	shook	shaken
drink	drank	drunk	show	showed	shown
drive	drove	driven	shut	shut	shut
eat	ate	eaten	sing	sang	sung
hear	heard	heard	sink	sank	sunk
fall	fell	fallen	sit	sat	sat
feed	fed	fed	sleep	slept	slept
feel	felt	felt	speak	spoke	spoken
find	found	found	spend	spent	spent
fly	flew	flown	stand	stood	stood
forget	forgot	forgotten	steal	stole	stolen
freeze	froze	frozen	stick	stuck	stuck
get	got	gotten/got	sweep	swept	swept
give	gave	given	swim	swam	swum
go	went	gone	take	took	taken
grow	grew	grown	teach	taught	taught
hit	hit	hit	tear	tore	torn
hold	held	held	tell	told	told
keep	kept	kept	think	thought	thought
know	knew	known	throw	threw	thrown
lay	laid	laid	wake	woke	woken
leave	left	left	wear	wore	worn
lend	lent	lent	win	won	won
lose	lost	lost	wind	wound	wound
make	made	made	write	wrote	written

There are three groups of conjunctions, each with specific rules for punctuation.

Coordinating Conjunctions

There are exactly seven coordinating conjunctions:

and

but

for (= because)

nor

or

so (= that's why)

yet (= but)

Use:

1. Join two independent clauses with a comma and a coordinating conjunction.

    Examples: Her family owns a small factory, and she manages it.
    This might look easy, but it's actually rather difficult.

2. If there isn't an independent clause after the coordinating conjunction, don't use a comma before it.

    Examples: Her family owns a small factory and is thinking of expanding.
    This looks easy but is actually rather difficult.

3. In a series of three or more nouns, adjectives, verbs, or phrases, use commas to separate each item; this structure occurs with *and* or *or*.

    Examples: We'll go to Tunisia, Morocco, or Egypt.
    Their business imports fabric, produces clothing, and sells the clothing locally.

Nor is used somewhat differently.

1. with different subjects:
   a. Alice won't go to Ghana this year, **nor** will John.
   b. Neither Alice nor John will go to Ghana this year.

2. with different verbs:
   a. Alice didn't call, nor did she write.
   b. Alice neither called nor wrote.

3. with different objects:
   a. John can't send a fax, nor can he send an e-mail.
   b. John can send neither a fax nor an e-mail.

Subordinating Conjunctions

These are some of the many subordinating conjunctions.

because	when	by the time
although	whenever	as soon as (= immediately after)
as (= because)	before	until
since (= because)	after	as (= while; when)
even though	while (= when)	
while (= although)		if
whereas		unless (= if not)
		in case

Use:

1. If you begin a sentence with a subordinating conjunction, use a comma to separate the dependent and independent clauses.

   Example: Because she wanted to do business in Asia, she studied Asian languages and culture.

2. If the subordinating conjunction is in the middle of the sentence, there is usually no comma.

   Example: She studied Asian languages and culture because she wanted to do business in Asia.

   Exception: There is often a comma before a subordinating conjunction of contrast.

   Example: The New Kingdom was a period of military success and power in Egypt, whereas the Old Kingdom had been a time of defeat and failure.

Adverbial Conjunctions (Conjunctive Adverbs)

These are some of the many adverbial conjunctions.

in addition moreover furthermore also	} = and	however neveltheless* even so*	} = but

in addition
moreover   } = and
furthermore
also

however
nevertheless*   } = but
even so*
(*Use these in a surprising situation.)

therefore
consequently
thus   } = that's why
as a result
for this reason

in contrast
on the other hand

for example   for instance
in other words   e.g.
that is
i.e.
                                 mostly
                                 for the most part
first   to some extent (= partly)
next   to a large extent (= mostly)
afterwards
finally   in short
then (no comma)   in conclusion

Use:

There are three main ways to use adverbial conjunctions: at the beginning of a sentence, at the beginning of an independent clause, or in the middle of an independent clause. Some conjunctions may appear at the end of a sentence.

Examples: The museum has an extensive collection of religious art. In addition, it houses a fine but small collection of genre paintings.

The exhibit of Egyptian art is extremely rare and valuable; consequently, security will be extraordinarily tight.

Everyone dreams every night. Many people, however, do not remember their dreams in the morning.

Everyone dreams every night. Many people do not remember their dreams in the morning, however.

Name: _____ **Date:** _____

Taking Notes on *International Culture*

Directions: Complete the graphic organizer below to take notes on *International Culture,* pages 11–12. For each topic, write down examples or details you find in the reading.

Section	Notes
Introduction	
Language	
Religion	
Values and Attitudes	
Customs and Manners	
Material Culture	

Editing Practice

Directions: There are at least seven mistakes in tense, modals, adjective clauses, punctuation, and coordinating conjunctions in the paragraph below. Find and correct them.

U.S. companies, that do business in Japan should to learn about the culture and language, and they will make the same mistakes others have made. For example, one company tries to sell a cake mix, that could be made in a Japanese rice cooker. No one bought it. The company didn't know that Japanese people only want to cook rice in a rice cooker. In Japan, steering wheels are usually on the right side of the car but when some Japanese buy foreign cars, they want the steering wheel on the left. The left-side steering wheel is higher status. In some parts of Europe, a *taverna* is a place to eat and drink. In Japanese, the expression *taberna* meant "do not eat." Knowing about Japanese culture and language can help U.S. companies avoid costly mistakes.

Editing Practice

Directions: There are at least six mistakes in punctuation, adverbial conjunctions, run-ons and comma splices, and the passive voice in the paragraph below. Find and correct them.

The San people of southern Africa represent a number of different tribes and languages. For the most part they are hunter-gatherers. Sometimes the San work for farmers and ranchers. However, after a long drought, resources are scarce the San return to hunting and gathering to make better use of the limited resources. In the past, conflict was sometimes create when farmers took land or water that the San hunter-gatherers considered their own, or when livestock is stolen by the hunter-gatherers for food. Sometimes an agreement reached when the hunter-gatherers received food and protection in exchange for working as livestock herders or as hunters. Governments sometimes allowed farmers and traders to attack the San who resisted, the number of hunter-gatherers was significantly reduced.

Outlining a Paragraph of Analysis

Directions: Complete the graphic organizer below to plan your paragraph of analysis.

Topic Sentence:

_____

    Supporting information:

      _____

        Specific detail 1:

        _____

        Specific detail 2:

        _____

    Supporting information:

      _____

        Specific detail 1:

        _____

        Specific detail 2:

        _____

    Supporting information:

      _____

        Specific detail 1:

        _____

        Specific detail 2:

        _____

Concluding Sentence:

_____

Name: _____ **Date:** _____

Religious Art Research

Directions: Use the Internet to search for five examples of art for the religion you are researching (Islamic, Hindu, Christian, etc.). Fill in the chart below.

Religion: _____

Name of the Piece of Art	Art Form (painting, sculpture, etc.)	Details (What's in it? What does it look like?)
Example 1:		
Example 2:		
Example 3:		
Example 4:		
Example 5:		

Comparing Paintings

Directions: Complete the Venn diagram below to compare and contrast a pair of paintings from page 90 or 91.

Painting 1:   **Painting 2:**

_____   _____

Both

Editing Practice

Directions: Read the paragraph below about the illustrations on page 86. There are at least ten mistakes in appositives, adjectives, participial phrases, prepositional phrases, adjectives, and transitional expressions of comparison-contrast in the paragraph. Find and correct them.

Both *John Brown Going to His Hanging* and the model depicting the counting of livestock from the tomb of Meketre present scenes from everyday life, but they have many more differences than similarities. In the two pieces of art, there are crowds of people and at least one building. In the model, only an Egyptian small building is center. There are many men watching and counted livestock. Similarly, in the painting of John Brown's hanging, there are several wooden buildings extend out to the side. Like the model, the people in the painting are facing away from the viewer. The background is very full in the painting. In the model, you can't see trees or other buildings. In the painting, John Brown the man in the center is about to be killed, creates a moment of drama and excitement. In contrast we can see a very ordinary activity in the model.

Cause and Effect Matching

Directions: Cut along the dotted lines. Mix up the slips of paper and match the causes and effects.

1. The *Palette of King Narmer* is called a palette	because it looks like the stone Egyptians used to mix cosmetics.
2. Narmer's lower body is seen in profile and his torso full front	since he is a king.
3. Artists were following the strict rules of powerful priests;	therefore, the flat artistic styles stayed the same for thousands of years.
4. The pharaoh is the largest figure	because he is the most important.
5. The painting shouldn't have empty spaces	so the background was filled with animals, plants, and hieroglyphs.
6. All important body parts must appear in the painting	so the person's spirit does not live forever without an arm or a leg.
7. Because several of the figures are low status	they can be in more natural positions.
8. We know that Egyptians were able to create realistic art	because there are examples, such as the portrait of Nefertiti.
9. We know a lot about ancient Egyptian life	because of excavations.
10. Since it has existed for thousands of years,	the Sphinx has lost part of its face.

Editing Practice

Directions: There are at least eight mistakes in infinitives of purpose, adjectives, subordinating conjunctions, and conjunctions of cause and effect in the paragraph below. Find and correct them.

Ancient Egyptians spent vast amounts of time and wealth on huge magnificent tombs protect their dead kings, however, grave robbers managed to break into most tombs and steal the fabulous contents. Therefore there was tremendous excitement when the tomb of Tutankhamen was discovered in 1922. The tomb had not been robbed, and as a result it was still filled with an almost unimaginable number of priceless objects, including the gold astonishing mask of the pharaoh himself. The richness of the tomb was also surprising because of "King Tut" he was just eighteen years old when he died and that he was considered an Egyptian minor king.

Name: _____ **Date:** _____

Text Connections

Directions: Read each section of *Lucid Dreaming* on pages 141–142 and make notes in the chart. For example, in the first row, Text to Self, write down any connections you can make between what you read (Text) and what you already know (Self). Under "The History of Lucid Dreaming," a student might write: *I often have dreams in which I know I am dreaming.*

Type of Connection	The History of Lucid Dreaming	Techniques for Developing Lucidity
Text to Self (Connection between what you read and your own experience)		
Text to Text (Connection between two different texts you read)		
Text to World (Connection between what you read and what you know about the world)		

Editing Practice

Directions: There are at least seven mistakes in punctuation, tenses, conjunctions of time, and expressions to explain symbols in the paragraph below. Find and correct them.

In my dream, I'm in a boat going down a river with my younger sister. The water is flowing very fast, and we were afraid. I realize that there are more rocks up ahead and that the boat will turn over. We might drown. When I steer the boat near the shore I make my little sister get out and swim. I keep go down the river. Water is often associated of life. I think the river is a symbol to life, and the rocks are symbolic with the possible dangers we face. I have always protected my little sister, and in the dream, I realize we have to live our own lives. When she swims to the side of the river, that symbolizes of her own independence. When I continue down the river, I decide to face my own future, whatever it is.

Graphic Organizer for *What is Abnormal?*

Directions: Complete the graphic organizer with key words and expressions from the reading *What is Abnormal?* on pages 173–175.

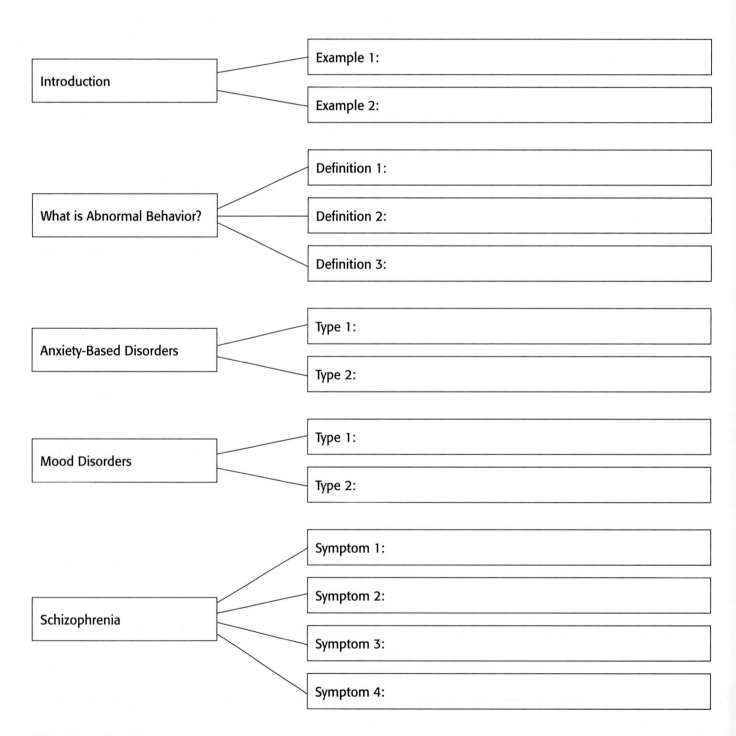

| Introduction | Example 1: |
| | Example 2: |

What is Abnormal Behavior?	Definition 1:
	Definition 2:
	Definition 3:

| Anxiety-Based Disorders | Type 1: |
| | Type 2: |

| Mood Disorders | Type 1: |
| | Type 2: |

Schizophrenia	Symptom 1:
	Symptom 2:
	Symptom 3:
	Symptom 4:

Editing Practice

Directions: Correctly rewrite the sentences below.

1. A disadvantage to drugs is that after leaving the hospital, patients might have problems with the real world. Soon he might be back in the hospital.

   _____

   _____

   _____

2. A drawback on some of the antidepressant drugs is that it has side effects.

   _____

   _____

3. A therapist practices behavior therapy sometimes have patients write a list of fears.

   _____

   _____

4. A principle of psychoanalysis is that patients can understand their own emotions, this understanding is called *insight*.

   _____

   _____

5. In Algeria, there is a disorder which the person is possess by evil spirits.

   _____

   _____

6. Self-help groups have been form to deal with alcoholism an addiction to alcohol.

   _____

   _____

Class Outline

Directions: Cut along the dotted lines and mix up the slips of paper. Work together to arrange the slips into an outline for the reading *Addiction: What Can Be Done About It?* on pages 214–215.

INTRODUCTION

Addiction: physiological or psychological dependence on a substance or activity.

Physiological dependence: body accustomed to drug; needs it to function

Tolerance: body needs larger doses for same effect

Withdrawal: painful physical symptoms when drug taken away

Psychological dependence: depend on feelings created by drug

INTERVENTION

Interrupting downward slide

Meeting with professional

Meeting with addict

RECOVERY

Recovery: learning to live without alcohol or drugs

Recognize problem

Decide to give drugs up

Detoxification

Abstinence

TREATMENT CHOICES

Support groups

Treatment centers

CODEPENDENCY

People who are not addicted but live with addict

Protect the addict from the consequences of behavior

Editing Practice

Directions: There are at least six errors in the paragraph below in the present unreal conditional, subordinating conjunctions, and fragments. Find and correct them.

Alcohol should not be advertised on television for several reasons. First, research suggests that children are affected by television advertising. For example, ads for sugary cereals. If children don't see so much alcohol advertised on television, they might not be influenced to try alcohol at a young age. Second, television commercials make the use of alcohol seem glamorous and attractive. If people didn't always see drinking alcohol as a positive activity, they will be more realistic about the problems of alcohol. Perhaps commercials for alcohol are not so widely shown on television, people will be less likely to use it. The government needs to pass laws to limit advertising for alcohol. Of course, the television industry would lose a lot of money by limiting advertising for alcohol. Because beer companies are among the top advertisers on TV.

Cause and Effect Chain

Directions: Reread the section "For a Happy Heart," pages 236–237. Complete the graphic organizer below to identify causes and effects related to stress and the body's response.

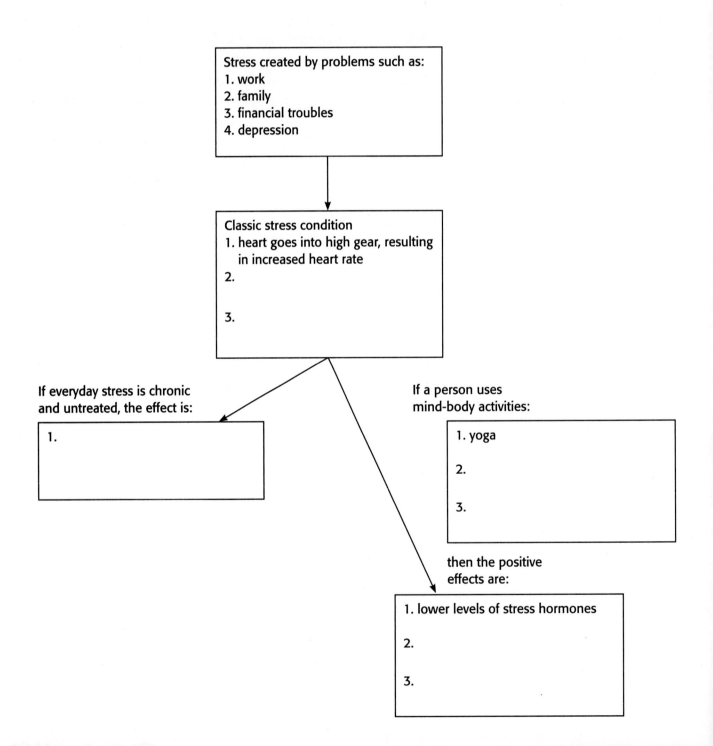

Stress created by problems such as:
1. work
2. family
3. financial troubles
4. depression

Classic stress condition
1. heart goes into high gear, resulting in increased heart rate
2.

3.

If everyday stress is chronic and untreated, the effect is:

1.

If a person uses mind-body activities:

1. yoga

2.

3.

then the positive effects are:

1. lower levels of stress hormones

2.

3.

Editing Practice

Directions: There are at least six errors in punctuation and conjunctions. Find and correct them.

According to Lynn Payer the author of Medicine and Culture European medicine is quite different from American medicine, for example, doctors in England are rather conservative. English doctors don't often give physical exams or prescribe drugs frequently. Because they believe that no treatment is better than incorrect and unnecessary treatment. While physicians in the United States focus on bacteria and other external causes of disease. French doctors believe that a patient's general physical condition is equally important. For this reason French doctors prescribe vitamins more often than antibiotics.

Name _____ **Date** _____ **Score** _____

○ Reading

Directions: Read the paragraph below. Then fill in the bubble of the correct answer for each comprehension question that follows.

In the book *The Geography of Thought: How Asians and Westerners Think Differently . . . and Why*, Richard E. Nisbett compares the ways that people from Asia see and think with the ways that Americans see and think. Basically, when Asians look at a picture, they notice objects in the front as well as the background. Americans often pay particular attention to the objects in front, or the ones they believe are important. Because of this, Americans don't always notice everything in the picture. If Americans see a photo of a fish swimming in a tank, they will see details on the fish, but they might not notice the plants in the background. The difference in how people see is similar to how they think. People from Asian countries are often very aware of the many factors (social hierarchy, for example) that can influence a business or social situation. Americans might say that Asians "can't see the forest for the trees." However, Americans often pay attention only to what they think is most important, and don't even notice specific details. When companies doing business in both Asia and the United States develop a marketing plan, they might want to consider the differences that Nisbett has noted.

1. What is the main idea of this passage?
   - Ⓐ Asians see details, but Americans see only the important objects or ideas.
   - Ⓑ Asians and Americans are different.
   - Ⓒ Asians are aware of social hierarchy.
   - Ⓓ Asians and Americans see and think in different ways.

2. Who is more likely to see small objects in a picture?
   - Ⓐ Asians
   - Ⓑ Americans
   - Ⓒ Both Asians and Americans
   - Ⓓ Neither Asians nor Americans

3. Who pays more attention to all the factors that might affect a situation?
   - Ⓐ Asians
   - Ⓑ Americans
   - Ⓒ Both Asians and Americans
   - Ⓓ Neither Asians nor Americans

4. What is a good explanation of the figure of speech "they can't see the forest for the trees"?

- Ⓐ There is too much wood in the picture.
- Ⓑ They can't see the whole picture because they are focused on the details.
- Ⓒ They can see the big ideas, but they can't see the small ones.
- Ⓓ They can't see each tree, and they can't see all of the trees.

5. What is an example of something that might affect a social situation?

- Ⓐ fish
- Ⓑ the background
- Ⓒ social hierarchy
- Ⓓ the marketing plan

○ Strategy: Making Inferences

Directions: For each sentence below, fill in the bubble next to the best inference.

6. Maria probably wishes she had asked her guests what foods they didn't like to eat.

- Ⓐ Maria served food that her guests didn't like.
- Ⓑ Maria asked her guests what they would like to eat.
- Ⓒ Maria should not have asked her guests what they would like to eat.

7. The picture on the American package was of a fish, so Miok bought it for lunch.

- Ⓐ Miok could not read English, but realized it was fish from the picture.
- Ⓑ Miok could read English.
- Ⓒ Miok liked to eat fish.

8. Indonesia is a collectivistic culture. In collectivist cultures, people think of themselves more as members of a group than as individuals.

- Ⓐ Most Indonesians prefer to gather in a group for decisions.
- Ⓑ Most Indonesians base decisions on the needs of the group.
- Ⓒ Most Indonesians base decisions on their own needs.

9. An American car in the 1970s was called the Nova. In Spanish nova means "doesn't go."

- Ⓐ The name might be a problem in Spanish-speaking countries.
- Ⓑ The car was very successful in Spanish-speaking countries.
- Ⓒ It is a good name for a car in Spanish-speaking countries.

10. Juan was late to work for five days in a row, so his boss fired Juan.

      (A) Juan didn't care about being late to his job.

      (B) The boss didn't like Juan.

      (C) Being on time was important.

○ Vocabulary

Directions: Complete each sentence with a word or phrase from the box.

adapt	avoid	costly	ignore	technology
appropriate	bow	hierarchy	risk	work ethic

11. I'm not good with _____. I can't even use a computer.

12. When Kim moved here, she had to _____ to our customs.

13. It's not a good idea to _____ the instructor when she gives you directions.

14. It was a _____ mistake—the company lost millions of dollars.

15. When Scott was in Korea, he learned to _____ when he met important people.

16. It's a big _____ to move to a new city, but you often are rewarded.

17. Mr. Tanner is my boss's boss. I guess he's at the top of the office _____.

18. You always come in early in the morning and stay late at night. You have a great _____.

19. Get some advice before you travel so you can _____ embarrassing mistakes.

20. Ken's behavior at the meeting was not _____, so his supervisor had a serious talk with him afterwards.

○ Mechanics

Directions: Complete the paragraph with the correct words in parentheses.

For Americans, being on time _____ (is/was) usually important. Employees
21
_____ (who/which) _____ (come/came) late to work _____ (should/ought)
22   **23**   **24**
to apologize and maybe give a reason for their lateness. The rules _____ (are/were) a little
25
different for social occasions. Often, Americans _____ (arrive/arrived) a few minutes late to
26
parties. My mother _____ (have/had) a dinner party when she first got married. She
27
_____ (tells/told) everyone to come at 7:00. By 7:25, no one had arrived, _____
28   **29**
(but/so) she _____ (is/was) very upset. Everyone came at 7:30!
30

○ Editing

Directions: Find and correct the five mistakes in tense, adjective clauses, and coordinating conjunctions.

Abercrombie and Fitch, a clothing company who operates in the United States, has ads who

picture beautiful young people. Sometimes the young women in the ads show their stomachs or

other parts of their bodies. These ads are acceptable in the United States, so they would not be

acceptable in many Muslim countries. However, some Abercrombie and Fitch ads are offensive to

people in the United States. In 2005, the company makes T-shirts with messages that seemed

sexist, or devaluing of women. A group of teenaged girls encourages others not to buy the

company's clothes.

Name _____ **Date** _____ **Score** _____

○ Reading

Directions: Read the textbook excerpt (part) below. Then fill in the bubble of the correct answer for each comprehension question that follows.

Capitalism and the U.S. Economy

A pure market or capitalist economic system has six major characteristics, or features: 1) little or no government control, 2) freedom of enterprise, 3) freedom of choice, 4) private property, 5) profit incentive, and 6) competition. These characteristics are interrelated and are all present in varying degrees in the U.S. economy.

The Role of Government. Many economists argue that pure capitalism has never existed. Capitalism in the United States today can be defined as an economic system in which private individuals own the factors of production and decide how to use them within the limits of the law. The Constitution limits the national government's control over economic activities, yet the role of government in the economy has greatly increased since the Constitution was written more than 200 years ago. For example, today, governmental agencies regulate the quality of food and drugs, watch over the nation's money and banking system, inspect workplaces for hazardous (dangerous) conditions, and act to stop damage to the environment. Government also uses tax money for social programs such as Medicare (medical insurance), education, and job training.

Freedom of Enterprise. The U.S. economy is also called the free enterprise system. This term means that individuals are free to own and control the factors of production. For example, if you decide to go into business for yourself, your abilities and resources will help you decide the good or service to produce, the quantity (how much), and the way to produce it. In short, you make your own decisions about your business. There are certain legal limits on freedom of enterprise; for instance, in most states, young adults must be 16 years of age before they can work.

Source: *Economics: Today and Tomorrow* (Miller)

1. What is the main idea of the second paragraph?

- Ⓐ Pure capitalism has never existed in the U.S.
- Ⓑ The government has a limited role, but it does regulate certain activities.
- Ⓒ The government controls the free enterprise system.
- Ⓓ The government uses tax money for social programs.

2. What is the free enterprise system?

    (A) the role of government

    (B) a system in which individuals are free to own and control the factors of production

    (C) legal limits, such as age limits for work

    (D) owning a business

3. Which of the following is **not** a topic in the passage?

    (A) the role of government

    (B) capitalism

    (C) freedom of enterprise

    (D) profit

4. What is one limit to freedom on enterprise?

    (A) You can't decide which good or service to provide.

    (B) The government limits the quantity.

    (C) The government limits the age of workers.

    (D) The government controls the factors of production.

5. What is an important role of government in free enterprise?

    (A) It regulates food and drugs.

    (B) It regulates prices.

    (C) It regulates production.

    (D) It regulates quantities.

◯ Strategy: Understanding Parts of Speech

Directions: For each sentence below, fill in the bubble next to the part of speech of the word in bold.

6. The job of a construction work is usually hard **labor**.

    (A) verb   (B) noun

7. Jeff **sipped** the tea before he spoke to the doctor.

    (A) verb   (B) noun

8. We bought a dog to help us **herd** the sheep.

    (A) verb   (B) noun

9. The **demand** for oil is high, so prices are, too.

    (A) verb   (B) noun

10. Did you have to **bribe** Tony to wash your car?

    (A) verb   (B) noun

○ Vocabulary

Directions: Complete each sentence with a word from the box.

command	determines	edible	last	noted
crops	domesticated	intervene	nomadic	resources

11. In a _____ economy, the government controls production.

12. When there is a long period without rain, the _____ are often affected negatively.

13. The last few years, Mike has been rather _____, moving from one city to another.

14. Fortunately, I _____ the license plate of the car who hit the ice cream truck.

15. The weather report didn't say how long these cold temperatures would _____, but I hope it's not long.

16. Her coworkers had a big argument, but Cynthia didn't want to _____.

17. Some flowers are _____, so people put them on cakes and in salads.

18. Many developing countries are rich in natural _____, but they don't have the infrastructure to take advantage of them yet.

19. Demand often _____ supply. For example, if more people want a particular product, companies may produce more.

20. Dogs and cats are _____ animals.

○ Mechanics

Directions: Complete the sentences with the correct words in parentheses.

21. Oil _____ (produces/is produced) in many countries in the Middle East.

22. Her daughter is having trouble in school. _____ (Therefore/However), she has a meeting with the teacher tomorrow.

23. Most countries have a mixed economy; _____ (even so/in other words), the economy has elements of both the command and the market systems.

24. Economic systems that _____ (based/are based) on customs, beliefs, and religion are known as traditional systems.

25. International businesspeople should _____ (study/be studied) the customs of various countries.

26. Prairie dogs _____ (bought/were bought by) the Japanese as pets.

27. Prairie dogs are a natural part of the environment in the Midwest; _____ (nevertheless/therefore), they were not welcomed by farmers.

28. Lawrence Durrell wanted to buy the house, _____ (but/however) he pretended that he didn't.

29. In a capitalist system, economic decisions are made in the marketplace; _____ (however/for example), buyers and sellers may bargain over prices.

30. At potlatches, gifts _____ (were provided/provided) to guests.

○ Editing

Directions: Find and correct the mistakes in the passive voice, adverbial conjunctions, run-ons, and comma splices. There is one mistake in each sentence.

31. Small children sometimes set up a table in front of their house, they sell lemonade.

32. Children whose lemonade stands located on a busy street will probably have a successful business on a hot summer day.

33. People see the pitchers of ice-cold lemonade there is usually a high demand.

34. Children learn to increase their profits by selling more than just lemonade, for example, they offer cookies and cake for sale, too.

35. There is a sudden rainstorm or a drop in temperature the business quickly closes up.

Name _____ Date _____ Score _____

Reading

Directions: Read the passage below. Then fill in the bubble of the correct answer for each comprehension question that follows.

Visionary Art

The recently recognized field known as visionary art is created by self-taught artists, those artists without any formal training in art. As such, visionary art does not grow out of traditional art forms, but is the work of individuals who are driven to express their original vision of the world through art. Visionary art is sometimes called "outsider" art because it is created by people outside the mainstream of the art world.

Visionary art and folk art are often grouped together. Although both often use similar materials and methods, many in the art world would argue visionary art is not the same as folk art. Folk art is art learned at an elder's knee, passed down from one generation to another. It is formed by tradition and often includes jewelry making, quilting, and painting. Visionary artists invent their own traditions, figuring out what will work as they go.

There have always been artists who worked outside the traditional art world, but visionary art has become more important to collectors and educators in the last few decades. In the United States, many visionary artists live in the Southeast. In 1990, fewer than 10 museums in the U.S. included significant collections of visionary or folk art. Today, more than 50 museums have collections of visionary art.

1. What is the best expression of the main idea of this passage?
- Ⓐ Visionary art is like folk art in its use of materials and methods.
- Ⓑ Visionary art is now in many more museums in the United States.
- Ⓒ Visionary art is created out of the artist's need to express a vision rather than from tradition.
- Ⓓ Visionary art is important to people who collect and teach about art.

2. Which of the following are major sub-topics in this reading?
- Ⓐ definition of visionary art, comparison to folk art, growth of the field
- Ⓑ description of outsider art, types of folk art, number of museums
- Ⓒ formal art training, importance of community, location of artists
- Ⓓ similarity of folk and visionary art, art education, art museums

3. What is folk art?

  Ⓐ art with human figures

  Ⓑ another word for visionary art

  Ⓒ art learned from family or community

  Ⓓ art created by outsiders

4. What is the best description of the author's point of view about visionary art?

  Ⓐ angry

  Ⓑ critical

  Ⓒ interested

  Ⓓ humorous

5. Which of the following is true?

  Ⓐ Both folk art and visionary art are traditional.

  Ⓑ Both are passed from parent to child.

  Ⓒ Folk art is taught at college.

  Ⓓ Folk art and visionary art often use the same materials and methods.

○ Strategy: Understanding Italics

Directions: For each italicized word or phrase below, fill in the bubble to identify the reason for the italics.

6. I saw *Mission Impossible* on TV last night.

  Ⓐ title   Ⓑ foreign word   Ⓒ emphasis

7. Janet and her mother had a little *tête-a-tête*, or talk, about her grades.

  Ⓐ title   Ⓑ foreign word   Ⓒ emphasis

8. The chef made *paella* for the party.

  Ⓐ title   Ⓑ foreign word   Ⓒ emphasis

9. The *Mona Lisa* hangs in the Louvre Museum in Paris.

  Ⓐ title   Ⓑ foreign word   Ⓒ emphasis

10. I can't believe he has a *kangaroo* for a pet!

  Ⓐ title   Ⓑ foreign word   Ⓒ emphasis

○ Vocabulary

Directions: Complete each sentence with a word from the box.

abolitionists	cattle	described	genre	illuminated
afterlife	cloak	funeral	halo	meditation

11. Although slavery existed in many parts of the United States during the 19th century, many people were _____.

12. _____ is another word for livestock.

13. Paolo's mother died last week, so he returned home for the _____.

14. Henry _____ the accident in detail to the police.

15. A _____ painting depicts scenes from everyday life.

16. In most religions there is a belief in the _____.

17. The night air was cold, so Martin pulled his _____ around him.

18. _____ can help you find a state of peace and calm.

19. During the Middle Ages, artists _____ the pages of books.

20. In many paintings, a saint or holy person is drawn with a _____.

○ Mechanics

Directions: Complete the paragraph with the correct words or phrases in parentheses.

The painting has a large central figure _____ (faced/facing) front. The woman
_____ (sat/sitting) in the center of the painting is Mona Lisa. She is
                21
_____ (smiled/smiling) a mysterious smile. Leonardo daVinci, the
                22
_____ (great/Italian) _____ (great/Italian) artist, uses a special
                23   24   25
technique _____ (called/calling) *sfumato*, in which the lines in the painting are not
                26
clear. The landscape _____ (on/in) the background is dreamlike. The horizon, or
                27

place where the sky and earth meet, _____ (on/in) the left is lower than the right.
                                              28

With certain details, such as the horizon, da Vinci seems to have made a mistake.

_____ (In contrast/In a similar way), his depiction of human flesh seems perfect.
         29

da Vinci created a work of art _____ (appreciated/appreciating) by people all over
                                          30

the world.

◯ Editing

Directions: Find and correct the five mistakes with adjectives, participial phrases, and prepositional phrases.

Two women wearing dark long dresses are walking in front of a church, facing the back of the

painting. One is carrying an umbrella. Three children are nearby, faced front. Of the background,

there are other people stood in different groups. Fences divide the painting into different sections.

The clothing and appearance of the streets and buildings suggest that this is a European centuries-

old street scene.

Name _____ Date _____ Score _____

Reading

Directions: Read the passage below. Then fill in the bubble of the correct answer for each comprehension question that follows.

High-Tech Pyramid

I. M. Pei, a Chinese-American architect born in 1917, has brought the past into the present. He recently designed and built a large pyramid much as the Egyptians did in the past. However, he used new high technology materials and processes. Pei's pyramid is the new main entrance to the Louvre Museum in Paris, France. The pyramid is made of the special high-strength glass walls. The see-through walls give the structure a sense of transparency and lightness. Pei's glass pyramid is the first modern addition to the Louvre, which was originally a palace for the kings of France.

The pyramid has been criticized by people who are puzzled by the unexpected combination of this high-tech pyramid and the surrounding nineteenth-century stone buildings in a traditional style. However, Pei felt the project was a chance to integrate artistic design with his commitment to urban renewal—a plan to renew the city and help it meet current needs. The new addition to the Louvre is built above a huge below-ground network of services and passages. Pei hoped to revitalize the Louvre and give it new life and energy. His goal was to make it easy for people to enter the Louvre and to make the Louvre a part of the life of present-day Paris.

Source: *Art in Focus* (Mittler)

1. What is the main idea of this passage?
   - Ⓐ Pei's glass pyramid is the first modern addition to the Louvre.
   - Ⓑ Pei brought the past into the present by building a large pyramid like the ancient Egyptians but with modern materials and processes.
   - Ⓒ The pyramid has been criticized because it doesn't fit in with the surrounding buildings.
   - Ⓓ Pei's pyramid is the new main entrance to the Louvre.

2. Who is I. M. Pei?
   - Ⓐ the director of the Louvre
   - Ⓑ an Egyptian who designed the pyramids for museums
   - Ⓒ an American architect who designed a new part of the Louvre
   - Ⓓ the director of urban renewal in Paris

3. Where is the high-tech pyramid?

    Ⓐ in Paris

    Ⓑ in Egypt

    Ⓒ behind the Louvre

    Ⓓ in the United States

4. What does urban renewal mean?

    Ⓐ new and advanced

    Ⓑ brought together

    Ⓒ high technology

    Ⓓ a plan to help the city meet its current needs

5. What is one difference between Pei's pyramid and the pyramids of ancient Egypt?

    Ⓐ the shape

    Ⓑ the materials

    Ⓒ The new pyramid is solid.

    Ⓓ The ancient pyramids had entrances.

◯ Strategy: Using Opposites

Directions: For each word in bold, underline the word or words that mean its opposite.

6. The walls in the new building are **transparent**, unlike walls that block the view and light.

7. The architect wanted an **innovative** design, not the more traditional look of the original building.

8. The **revitalization** of the inner city brought hope to residents discouraged by the previous decay of buildings and services.

9. Archaeologists consider the pyramids of Egypt and Latin America to be engineering **marvels**. Most buildings of their time were simpler and plainer.

10. **Artisans** often received more money and respect than did unskilled workers.

◯ Vocabulary

Directions: Fill in the bubble for the word or phrase that best completes each sentence.

11. In Egyptian art, the face is shown in _____, or from the side.

    Ⓐ torso   Ⓑ profile   Ⓒ pose

12. Egypt wasn't the only country to have _____; China is known for its families that ruled for hundreds of years.

    Ⓐ dynasties   Ⓑ pharaohs   Ⓒ commoners

13. I've always wanted to have a house on a _____ because of the beautiful view.
   Ⓐ cemetery   Ⓑ dump   Ⓒ cliff

14. Some animals are _____ —they have only one partner for life.
   Ⓐ massive   Ⓑ magnificent   Ⓒ monogamous

15. Part of Mark's job is to _____ works of art to their original condition.
   Ⓐ pose   Ⓑ decree   Ⓒ restore

16. I have had a _____ of bad apartments. I hope my next one is better.
   Ⓐ succession   Ⓑ dynasty   Ⓒ continuity

17. Anna's last job was extremely difficult; it really _____ her health.
   Ⓐ took a toll on   Ⓑ put up with   Ⓒ kept up with

18. I think it would be hard to drive a _____ .
   Ⓐ vizier   Ⓑ falcon   Ⓒ chariot

19. Where did you get that dress? What a _____!
   Ⓐ pose   Ⓑ find   Ⓒ cloak

20. Tammy's not good with change—she really likes _____ .
   Ⓐ effects   Ⓑ stability   Ⓒ frozen

○ Mechanics

Directions: Combine the sentences using the words or phrases in parentheses. If necessary, change the order of the clauses to make your new sentences logical.

21. The stones were very large. Many people were needed to put the stones in place. (because)

_____

_____

22. The pharaoh had high status. Artists made the pharaoh the largest figure in the painting. (because of)

_____

_____

23. The instructor subtracted 15 points from Mark's paper. He handed it in late. (for)

_____

_____

24. Worker performance has improved dramatically. The new building is a much more attractive and stimulating place to work. (consequently)

_____

_____

25. He went to the post office. He bought stamps. (to)

_____

_____

26. Marie is really interested in archaeology. She has decided to major in it when she goes to college. (so)

_____

_____

27. The teacher is giving another test. The grades were poor on the first test. (due to)

_____

_____

28. Relatives wanted their loved ones to be protected in the afterlife. They buried food and objects in the tombs. (since)

_____

_____

29. You want to improve your writing. You should write a little every day. (to)

_____

_____

30. People from all over the world travel to Egypt. They go to the pyramids. (to)

_____

_____

○ Editing

Directions: Find and correct the five mistakes in infinitives of purpose, transitional expressions, subordinating conjunctions, and conjunctions of cause and effect.

The Metropolitan Museum in New York City has a famous collection of Egyptian art. In the early 20th century, the museum's board of directors established an Egyptian Expedition carry out archaeological excavations along the Nile River to add to the museum's collection. At that time, the waters of Lake Nasser rose due the building of the Aswan High Dam; consequently the Temple of Dendur was dismantled to saving it. Today, the Temple of Dendur from the 15th century B.C.E. is one of the most popular features of the museum. The Roman emperor Augustus built the Temple of Dendur in the 15th century B.C.E. to honor the Egyptian goddess Isis and the two sons of a local Nubian ruler because of they had helped the Romans in battle.

Name _____ **Date** _____ **Score**

○ Reading

Directions: Read the excerpt (part) from a magazine article below. Then fill in the bubble of the correct answer for each comprehension question that follows.

Nightmares and Other Dream Disorders

Dreams seem to be necessary for our mental functioning, but they are not always peaceful. There are several dreaming disorders that can upset the dreamer. Perhaps the most well-known dreaming disorder is the nightmare. Nightmares are vivid, frightening dreams that wake the dreamer from REM sleep. Most dreamers recall detailed but strange plots, or storylines. Almost half of the college students in one study reported at least one nightmare in a two-week period. Some medications can increase the incidence of nightmares. Two other dreaming disorders are REM behavior disorders and night terrors. People who suffer from REM behavior disorders are often middle-aged men. They experience vivid, violent, action-filled dreams that may cause them to act out in their sleep, sometimes resulting in injury to themselves or a partner. Night terrors usually affect children between the ages of 4 and 12. These episodes are filled with fear and panic, and the dreamer may cry out during sleep. Unlike nightmares, night terrors do not usually wake the dreamer. In fact, the dreamer is hard to arouse and usually cannot remember much of the dream.

1. What is the topic sentence of this paragraph?
   - Ⓐ Dreams seem to be necessary for our mental functioning, but they are not always peaceful.
   - Ⓑ There are several dreaming disorders that can upset the dreamer.
   - Ⓒ Nightmares are vivid, frightening dreams that wake the dreamer from REM sleep.
   - Ⓓ In fact, the dreamer is hard to arouse and usually cannot remember much of the dream.

2. Which dreaming disorder can cause violent actions during sleep?
   - Ⓐ nightmares
   - Ⓑ REM behavior disorders
   - Ⓒ night terrors
   - Ⓓ all of the above

3. According to the reading, what can increase nightmares?

     Ⓐ violent movies

     Ⓑ age

     Ⓒ medication

     Ⓓ crying

4. Which disorder often affects young children?

     Ⓐ nightmares

     Ⓑ REM behavior disorders

     Ⓒ night terrors

     Ⓓ all of the above

5. What is one way in which night terrors differ from nightmares?

     Ⓐ Night terrors are a dreaming disorder.

     Ⓑ Dreamers often scream during night terrors.

     Ⓒ Only young people have night terrors.

     Ⓓ Dreamers wake up during night terrors.

○ Strategy: Choosing the Correct Dictionary Definition

Directions: Fill in the bubble for the correct definition of each word in bold.

6. The dreamers can recall detailed **plots**.

     Ⓐ the events that form the story

     Ⓑ a secret plan you make with other people

     Ⓒ a small piece of land

7. There are several dreaming disorders that can **upset** the dreamer.

     Ⓐ make someone unhappy

     Ⓑ make someone sick

     Ⓒ change a plan

8. In fact, the dreamer is hard to **arouse**, and usually cannot remember much of the dream.

     Ⓐ cause a particular feeling in

     Ⓑ cause to stand upright

     Ⓒ wake someone up

9. Most dreamers **recall** detailed, strange plots, or storylines.

      Ⓐ to remember

      Ⓑ to ask people to return a product because of a problem

      Ⓒ to rearrange the order of something

10. They experience vivid, violent, action-filled dreams that may cause them to act out in their sleep, sometimes resulting in injury to themselves or a **partner**.

      Ⓐ a person with whom you do an activity, such as tennis

      Ⓑ one of the owners of a business

      Ⓒ one of two people who are married or live together

○ Vocabulary

Directions: Complete each sentence with a word or phrase from the box.

at random	disguise	ill will	overt	significance
cure	heal	in a panic	sacrifice	sufficient

11. I didn't know who he was because he wore a great _____.

12. Sometimes the meaning of a dream is not _____; the meaning may be hidden in the symbols in the dream.

13. It took a long time for his cut to _____, but it is finally better.

14. The winners of the prizes were chosen _____.

15. You don't have _____ money in your account, so I can't cash your check.

16. William was _____ when he couldn't find his wallet.

17. What is the _____ of money in dreams?

18. A good night's sleep can _____ almost any problem.

19. In some cultures, people believe that feelings of _____ can be changed to positive feelings by controlling dreams.

20. He had to _____ a lot to move to this country, but it was all worth it.

○ Mechanics

Directions: Complete the paragraph with the correct words or phrases in parentheses.

I had a terrible nightmare last night. At first, I was crawling in some grass. _____ **21** (Then/While) I was knocking on the door to a strange house. I saw a very old man _____ **22** (before/when) the door opened. He _____ **23** (led/leads) me into a large room. Lions _____ **24** (are/were) playing in front of a fireplace. _____ **25** (As/After) I was watching, the lions began to attack each other. The old man _____ **26** (disappears/disappeared). I was very afraid. _____ **27** (After/While) he disappeared, the lions saw me and started to run towards me. _____ **28** (Before/As soon as) I saw them come in my direction, I ran towards the door. The lions were _____ **29** (get/getting) closer and closer. My heart was pounding. _____ **30** (When/Then) I woke up.

○ Editing

Directions: Find and correct the ~~five~~ eleven errors in tense, conjunctions of time, and expressions used to explain symbols. Punctuation–

In his nightmare, the young man is trapped in a cave. There are many tunnels that lead out of the cave. First he went down one of the tunnels. The tunnel comes to a sudden end. Then he continues exploring the tunnels one by one. At the end of each one, the young man finds a blank wall. Second, he goes down the last tunnel. As he reaches the end, he fell into a deep hole. That's when he wakes up. The young man thinks the dream symbolizes of his panic at making a decision about a career.

Name _____ **Date** _____ **Score** _____

○ Reading

Directions: Read the textbook excerpt (part) below. Then fill in the bubble of the correct answer for each comprehension question that follows.

What Causes Schizophrenia?

Depression we can understand. Anxiety most of us have experienced. A person with schizophrenia, however, has such irrational behavior that it is hard for us to understand. The person withdraws from normal life and lives in a fantastic world that is full of fears. Schizophrenia is not a single problem; it does not have a single cause or cure. Rather, it is a collection of behaviors that show that a person has serious problems trying to meet the demands of life. What is the actual cause of schizophrenia? Most probably, the cause is an interaction of genetic, biochemical, and environmental factors.

Biological Factors. Genetics—the transmission of traits from parents to a child—is almost certainly a factor. As the degree of genetic relationship increases, so does the chance that if one member of a pair of humans develops schizophrenia, the other will too. Yet, among identical twins (twins born from the same egg), if one twin develops schizophrenia, there is only a 42 percent chance the other twin will develop it. This finding argues that other factors in addition to genetics also have a role.

Biochemical Factors. The proper working of the brain depends on the presence of the right amounts of many different chemicals, from oxygen to proteins. Some psychologists believe that psychological problems are due to chemical imbalances in the brain. Certain chemicals are not present in the right amount.

Environmental Factors. From Freud on, it has been tempting to blame the family situation in childhood for problems that people develop during adulthood. Paul Meehl (1962, 1989) suggests that bad experiences during childhood are not enough to lead to schizophrenia. However, it is true that being part of a pathogenic, or unhealthful, family may contribute to problems in the adult years.
    Explaining the causes of schizophrenia is perhaps the most complex research problem psychologists face.

Source: *Understanding Psychology* (Kasschau)

1. What is the main idea of this passage?

   (A) Schizophrenia is hard to understand.

   (B) Schizophrenia is caused by an interaction of genetic, biochemical, and environmental factors.

   (C) Schizophrenia is a collection of behaviors that show that a person has serious problems.

   (D) Schizophrenia is like depression and anxiety.

2. What is an example of a biological factor contributing to the development of schizophrenia?

   (A) The parents abused the child.

   (B) The brain did not have enough of a particular protein.

   (C) Both identical twins developed schizophrenia.

   (D) The patient had severe anxiety.

3. Which is an example of an environmental factor?

   (A) The parents abused the child.

   (B) The brain did not have enough of a particular protein.

   (C) Both identical twins developed schizophrenia.

   (D) The patient had severe anxiety.

4. How can professionals determine that a person has schizophrenia?

   (A) by testing the chemicals in the brain

   (B) by analyzing the family history

   (C) by looking at the patient's genes

   (D) by observing behaviors that indicate specific problems in dealing with life

5. What word probably best describes a person with schizophrenia?

   (A) depressed

   (B) anxious

   (C) fearful

   (D) bad

○ Strategy: Understanding Connotation

Directions: For each word or phrase in bold below, identify the connotation and fill in the correct bubble.

6. I think that idea is **nuts**.

   (A) Positive   (B) Neutral   (C) Negative

7. His behavior has been a little **abnormal**.

   (A) Positive   (B) Neutral   (C) Negative

8. Ben had a little too much to drink last night. He was **feeling no pain**.

      Ⓐ Positive   Ⓑ Neutral   Ⓒ Negative

9. I drank too much myself. I was too **drunk** to drive.

      Ⓐ Positive   Ⓑ Neutral   Ⓒ Negative

10. When people drink too much, they become **intoxicated**.

      Ⓐ Positive   Ⓑ Neutral   Ⓒ Negative

⭘ Vocabulary

Directions: Complete each sentence with a word or phrase from the box.

agoraphobia	anonymous	dizziness	irrational	outburst
amnesia	distinguish	free association	motive	severe

11. People who don't want to go to public places have _____.

12. Behavior is called _____ when it doesn't seem reasonable.

13. Psychoanalysts often use _____ in their therapy.

14. When people can't _____ between what is real and what is not, they may have schizophrenia.

15. Someone just gave a million dollars to the college, but she wants to remain _____ so they're not releasing her name.

16. The cashier called the security service because a customer had a violent _____ at the cash register.

17. After the accident, Linda had temporary _____, but now she can remember what happened.

18. I'm trying to figure out why Josh did that. I just don't understand his _____.

19. Some medications can cause _____, so you shouldn't drive after taking them.

20. Everyone gets depressed, but when depression is _____, you should see a professional.

○ Mechanics

Directions: Complete the paragraph with the correct words or phrases in parentheses.

A patient _____ (brought/was brought) to the hospital last night. He was
        21

_____ (having/had) violent outbursts. _____ (However/In addition), he
    22   **23**

seemed to be in a panic. He _____ (expressed/was expressed) many fears.
                               24

_____ (On the other hand/Moreover), he misunderstood what the hospital staff were
    25

doing and saying. He _____ (hospitalized/was hospitalized) and treated immediately for
               26

schizophrenia. The patient is calm and quiet this morning. _____ (However/Moreover),
                                 27

he will not _____ (release/be released) yet. The psychiatrist _____ (wants/is
     28   **29**

wanted) to see how the patient responds to the medication. _____ (On the other
                                   30

hand/Moreover), she'd like to find out more about his living situation.

○ Editing

Directions: Find and correct the five mistakes in the passive voice, adjective clauses, and adverbial conjunctions of contradiction.

Cognitive behavioral therapy is a form of psychological therapy that bases on the ways in that

our thinking affects how we feel and what we do. Therapists which use this approach help their

patients replace the ways of thinking that are causing problems. One benefit to this approach is

that we can change our thoughts much more easily than we can change a situation. In CBT, people

are encouraged to remain calm in bad situations. We will always have bad situations; however when

we become upset about the situation, we have two problems rather than one. Remaining calm is

avoided one of those problems.

Name _____ **Date** _____ **Score** _____

○ Reading

Directions: Read the textbook excerpt (part) below. Then fill in the bubble of the correct answer for each comprehension question that follows.

Codependency

Being overly concerned with other people's problems and feeling driven to fix those problems is known as codependency. People who show this kind of behavior are called codependents. They often live with or are close to alcoholics and drug addicts. Their codependency is sometimes referred to as co-addiction.

One of the most common traits of codependency is enabling. This means trying to protect the   5
person having trouble with alcohol or drugs from facing the consequences of his or her drug-related problems. Codependent people enable an addict by lying for the other person; lending the other person money, which may be used to purchase more drugs or alcohol; or making excuses for him or her. Enabling is not healthful caring. It just makes it easier for the addict to keep on drinking or using drugs.   10

Addiction as a Family Disease

In a family where there is alcoholism or other drug dependence, both addicts and codependent family members are suffering and need help. That is why alcoholism and drug dependence are sometimes referred to as family diseases. They affect everyone in the family. People in a family with drug or alcohol dependency experience terrible shame, fear, disappointment, guilt, and anger. They are embarrassed to admit these feelings, because they don't realize that millions of other   15
families suffer from the effects of drug dependency. Family members make the alcoholic or drug addict the center of their lives. They adjust their needs, emotions, and behaviors to the unhealthy demands, behaviors, and emotions of the addicted person. In the process they, too, often become unhealthy.

Source: *Health: A Guide to Wellness* (Merki and Merki)

1. What is the main idea of the third paragraph?

      (A) Everyone in an alcoholic's family gets sick.

      (B) Living with an addict can be unhealthy.

      (C) If one person in a family is addicted, it's more likely the others are, too.

      (D) People who live with an addict feel alone.

2. What is the best definition of *enabling*?

    Ⓐ It is one of the most common traits of codependency.

    Ⓑ It is not healthful caring.

    Ⓒ It is trying to protect the addict from the consequences of the drug or alcohol use.

    Ⓓ It makes it easier for the addict to keep using.

3. Why don't family members admit their feelings?

    Ⓐ They think they are unusual.

    Ⓑ They know millions of other families suffer the effects, too.

    Ⓒ They aren't affected.

    Ⓓ They think it is the dependent person's problem.

4. What is the term for people who are overly concerned about the problems of someone else?

    Ⓐ an addict

    Ⓑ a dependent

    Ⓒ a codependent

    Ⓓ enabling

5. Which of the following is *not* an enabling behavior?

    Ⓐ lying

    Ⓑ lending money

    Ⓒ making excuses

    Ⓓ arranging an intervention

○ Strategy: Finding Sentences with Similar Meanings

Directions: For each sentence below, find the sentence in the passage that has a similar meaning. Then fill in the bubble next to the line number of the correct sentence.

6. When you don't allow an addict to face the problems caused by his addiction, you are enabling.

    Ⓐ (3)   Ⓑ (5)   Ⓒ (9)

7. Family members may be reluctant to talk about their feelings because they think they are the only ones facing this problem.

    Ⓐ (10)   Ⓑ (13)   Ⓒ (15)

8. Family members develop problems as they try to meet the demands of the addict.

    Ⓐ (6)   Ⓑ (14)   Ⓒ (18)

9. Family members help the addict continue his addiction when they make excuses, lie, or lend the addict money.

    Ⓐ (4)   Ⓑ (7)   Ⓒ (14)

10. Alcoholism is a family disease because everyone in the family is affected.

       Ⓐ (11)   Ⓑ (13)   Ⓒ (16)

○ Vocabulary

Directions: Complete each sentence with a word or phrase from the box.

abstinence confidential	craved culinary	epidemic inhalant	negligible relapse	rely on transmission

11. A recovering addict should practice total _____ .

12. Medical experts predict another global _____ of a form of flu.

13. There was a _____ amount of food left, so we threw it out.

14. I really _____ some ice cream, so we stopped on the way home.

15. Doctors cannot give out _____ patient information.

16. Tony is going to _____ school because he wants to cook in a restaurant.

17. I can really _____ my parents; they are dependable.

18. The sharing of needles used to inject drugs led to the _____ of HIV and AIDS.

19. Robin had been sober for two years, but she had a _____ and is drinking again.

20. Glue is an _____ used by many teenagers.

○ Mechanics

Directions: Restate each real situation in a sentence using *if* and the present unreal conditional.

21. Because I have a new job, I make more money.

_____

22. He smokes a lot so he often gets sick.

_____

23. We can't eat there because we don't have reservations.

_____

24. I am sober now because I belong to Alcoholics Anonymous.

_____

25. Since heroin is often injected, the health risks are great.

_____

26. Tobacco is not controlled effectively, so cigarette use is increasing in developing countries.

_____

27. I don't study enough, so I make poor grades.

_____

28. We are at the beach today because the weather is so beautiful.

_____

29. People live longer now because health care is good.

_____

30. Because you smoke, you are 15 times more likely to get lung cancer.

_____

○ Editing

Directions: Find and correct the five mistakes in subordinating conjunctions, fragments, and the present unreal conditional.

In the U.S., the tobacco industry is a wealthy and powerful group. However, it is time the government did more to regulate tobacco or make it illegal, since many people would protest such controls on their cigarettes. If tobacco was illegal, it will be much harder for young people to begin smoking. Also, more smokers will be motivated to quit. Unless we take strong action. People will continue to become addicted.

Name _____ **Date** _____ **Score** _____

○ Reading

Directions: Read the passage from an exercise class brochure below. Then fill in the bubble of the correct answer for each comprehension question that follows.

Health Benefits of Tai Chi

   Tai chi is a relatively gentle form of exercise that has many health benefits, especially for older people. Although tai chi has its roots in martial arts like karate and judo, its movements are fluid and not jarring to the joints. Similar to yoga, tai chi focuses on deep breathing and inner awareness. Our classes usually begin with breathing exercises, followed by gentle stretching. Participants in classes often review previously learned movements, adding new ones. Then all movements are joined together in a smoothly flowing form.

   Because tai chi involves controlled movement and balance, it can increase flexibility and improve strength in the muscles used for posture and balance. Tai chi has also been shown to help reduce blood pressure and enhance cardiovascular health in general. Its slow, weight-shifting movements can help increase bone strength. Many participants report improvements in psychological health, including relaxation, calmness, and a feeling of well-being. If you are interested, please attend one of our classes.

1. What is the main idea of this passage?
   - Ⓐ Tai chi is beneficial for both physical and psychological health.
   - Ⓑ Tai chi is a simple, gentle form of exercise.
   - Ⓒ Tai chi can increase flexibility, improve strength, and enhance cardiovascular health.
   - Ⓓ Through tai chi, participants become relaxed and calm.

2. What is the purpose of this passage?
   - Ⓐ to describe how tai chi is done
   - Ⓑ to give the history of tai chi
   - Ⓒ to persuade people to try tai chi
   - Ⓓ to compare tai chi to other forms of exercise

3. What is the tone of the passage?
  - (A) critical of tai chi
  - (B) uncertain
  - (C) neutral
  - (D) positive toward tai chi

4. How does a tai chi class usually begin?
  - (A) gentle stretching
  - (B) deep breathing
  - (C) review of learned movements
  - (D) introduction of new movements

5. Which of the following also focuses on inner awareness?
  - (A) judo
  - (B) karate
  - (C) weight lifting
  - (D) yoga

○ Strategy: Hedging

Directions: For each sentence below, fill in the bubble of the sentence that uses hedging.

6.
  - (A) The results of some studies suggest that meditation is beneficial to your health.
  - (B) Studies show that meditation is beneficial to your health.

7.
  - (A) Yoga is great for your mind and body.
  - (B) Many people report that yoga is great for mind and body.

8.
  - (A) Everyone should practice tai chi to improve mind-body health.
  - (B) Tai chi may be one way to improve mind-body health.

9.
  - (A) It's possible that you can use your mind to improve your physical health.
  - (B) One way to improve physical health is by using your mind.

10.
  - (A) If patients rely on mind-body medicine, they will not take advantage of conventional medicine.
  - (B) One possible drawback to mind-body medicine may be that patients will not take advantage of conventional medicine.

○ Vocabulary

Directions: Complete each sentence with a word or phrase from the box.

baffling	device	hypertension	obesity	quack
chronic	hostility	integrate	placebo	wear down

11. When the physician found out how high Michael's blood pressure was, she diagnosed him with
_____ .

12. The increase in _____ in the United States may, in part, be a result of how much fast food Americans consume.

13. Many patients improve with some kind of treatment, even when given a _____ .

14. _____ back pain is a problem for many older adults.

15. Stress can _____ your body's ability to fight illness.

16. Feelings of _____ can increase your blood pressure and heart rate.

17. His symptoms were _____ , so the doctors had difficulty diagnosing his problem.

18. Some patients with cancer are so hopeless that they turn to any _____ who can offer a cure, however crazy.

19. A pace-maker is a _____ that helps regulate the heart.

20. Many medical practitioners _____ conventional medicine with complementary techniques.

○ Mechanics

Directions: Complete the paragraph with the correct words or phrases in parentheses.

Yoga _____21_____ (may/must) be a good way to reduce stress. People who

practice yoga get the benefits of exercise, _____22_____ (so/but) without

the jarring of fragile joints such as knees. In yoga, you practice a special type of breathing.

_____23_____ (As a result/Nevertheless), you can stay relaxed even when exercising.

_____24_____ (Since/Although) many people feel the effects of yoga right away,

for others, the results _____25_____ (could not/might not) be immediate.

_____26_____ (However/Thus), most people will get some benefit if they stick with it.

In addition to breath control, yoga often involves repetitive actions, _____27_____

(but/so) it can produce a meditative state. Some people may have physical problems that prevent

them from vigorous exercise. _____28_____ (Consequently/Even so), they

_____29_____ (will/can) practice some simple yoga positions and yoga breathing.

There are even classes for people who _____30_____ (must/could) remain seated

because they can't stand.

○ Editing

Directions: Find and correct the five mistakes in modals of possibility, conjunctions, quotations, and italics.

Dr. Herbert Benson has written a number of books, including "The Relaxation Response." Dr.

Benson, in studies at Harvard, found that just as activity in one part of the brain can activate the 'fight

or flight response', activating other parts of the brain can reduces stress and relax the body. He

suggests that repeating a word or an activity, for consciously ignoring distracting thoughts and stimuli,

will activate these other parts of the brain. Even so, this process causes a "relaxation response."

Chapter 1 Test

Reading

1. D; 2. A; 3. A; 4. B; 5. C

Strategy: Making Inferences

6. A; 7. C; 8. B; 9. A; 10. C

Vocabulary

11. technology; 12. adapt; 13. ignore; 14. costly;
15. bow; 16. risk; 17. hierarchy; 18. work ethic;
19. avoid; 20. appropriate

Mechanics

21. is; 22. who; 23. come; 24. ought; 25. are;
26. arrive; 27. had; 28. told; 29. so; 30. was

Editing

Abercrombie and Fitch, a clothing company
~~who~~ ^that^ operates in the United States, has ads
~~who~~ ^that^ picture beautiful young people.
Sometimes the young women in the ads
show their stomachs or other parts of their
bodies. These ads are acceptable in the
United States, ~~so~~ ^but^ they would not be
acceptable in many Muslim countries.
However, some Abercrombie and Fitch ads
are offensive to people in the United States.
In 2005, the company ~~makes~~ ^made^ T-shirts with
messages that seemed sexist, or devaluing to
women. A group of teenaged girls encourage^d^
others not to buy the company's clothes.

Chapter 2

Reading

1. A; 2. B; 3. D; 4. C; 5. A

Strategy: Understanding Parts of Speech

6. B; 7. A; 8. A; 9. B; 10. A

Vocabulary

11. command; 12. crops; 13. nomadic; 14. noted;
15. last; 16. intervene; 17. edible; 18. resources;
19. determines; 20. domesticated

Mechanics

21. is produced; 22. Therefore; 23. in other words;
24. are based; 25. study; 26. were bought by;
27. nevertheless; 28. but; 29. for example;
30. were provided

Editing (Answers may vary.)

31. Small children sometimes set up a table
in front of their house, ^and^ they sell
lemonade.

32. Children whose lemonade stands ^are^
located on a busy street will probably
have a successful business on a hot
summer day.

33. ^When p^People see the pitchers of ice-cold
lemonade ^,^ there is usually a high
demand.

34. Children learn to increase their profits by
selling more than just lemonade ^; ^for
example, they offer cookies and cake for
sale, too.

35. ^When t^There is a sudden rainstorm or a
drop in temperature ^,^ the business
quickly closes up.

Chapter 3

Reading

1. C; 2. A; 3. C; 4. C; 5. D

Strategy: Understanding Italics

6. A; 7. B; 8. B; 9. A; 10. C

Vocabulary

11. abolitionists; 12. cattle; 13. funeral;
14. described; 15. genre; 16. afterlife; 17. cloak;
18. meditation; 19. illuminated; 20. halo

Mechanics

21. facing; 22. sitting; 23. smiling; 24. great;
25. Italian; 26. called; 27. in; 28. on; 29. In contrast;
30. appreciated

Editing

Two women wearing (dark) long dresses are walking in front of a church, facing the back of the painting. One is carrying an umbrella. Three children are nearby, ~~faced~~ ^facing^ front. ~~Of~~ ^In^ the background, there are other people ~~stood~~ ^standing^ in different groups. Fences divide the painting into different sections.

The clothing and appearance of the streets and buildings suggest that this is a (European)/centuries-old street scene.

Chapter 4

Reading

1. B; 2. C; 3. A; 4. D; 5. B

Strategy: Using Opposites

6. block view and light; 7. traditional; 8. decay;
9. buildings…simpler and plainer; 10. unskilled workers

Vocabulary

11. B; 12. A; 13. C; 14. C; 15. C; 16. A; 17. A; 18. C;
19. B; 20. B

Mechanics

21. Because the stones were very large, many people were needed to put the stones in place.
22. Because of the pharaoh's high status, artists made him the largest figure in the painting.
23. The instructor subtracted 15 points from Mark's paper, for he handed it in late.
24. The new building is a much more attractive and stimulating place to work; consequently, worker performance has improved dramatically.
25. He went to the post office to buy stamps.
26. Marie is really interested in archaeology, so she has decided to major in it when she goes to college.
27. The teacher is giving another test due to the poor grades on the first test.
28. Since relatives wanted their loved ones to be protected in the afterlife, they buried food and objects in the tombs.
29. You should write a little every day to improve your writing.
30. People from all over the world travel to Egypt to go to the pyramids.

Editing

The Metropolitan Museum in New York City has a famous collection of Egyptian art. In the early 20th century, the museum's board of directors established an Egyptian Expedition ^to^ carry out archaeological excavations along the Nile River to add to the museum's collection. At that time, the waters of Lake Nasser rose due ^to^ the building of the Aswan High Dam; consequently ^∧^ the Temple of Dendur was dismantled to ~~saving~~ ^save^ it. Today, the Temple of Dendur from the 15th century B.C.E is one of the most popular features of the museum. The Roman emperor Augustus built the Temple of Dendur in the 15th century B.C.E to honor the Egyptian goddess Isis and the two sons of a local Nubian ruler because ~~of~~ they had helped the Romans in battle.

Chapter 5
Reading
1. B; 2. B; 3. C; 4. C; 5. B

Strategy: Choosing the Correct Dictionary Definition
6. A; 7. A; 8. C; 9. A; 10. C

Vocabulary
11. disguise; 12. overt; 13. heal; 14. at random;
15. sufficient; 16. in a panic; 17. significance;
18. cure; 19. ill will; 20. sacrifice

Mechanics
21. Then; 22. when; 23. led; 24. were; 25. As;
26. disappeared; 27. After; 28. As soon as;
29. getting; 30. Then

Editing

In his nightmare, the young man is trapped in a cave. There are many tunnels that lead out of the cave. First ∧ he ~~went~~ ^goes^ down one of the tunnels. The tunnel comes to a sudden end. Then he continues exploring the tunnels one by one. At the end of each one, the young man finds a blank wall. ~~Second,~~ ^Finally^ ∧ he goes down the last tunnel. As he reaches the end, he ~~fell~~ ^falls^ ∧ into a deep hole. That's when he wakes up. The young man thinks the dream symbolizes ~~of~~ his panic at making a decision about a career.

Chapter 6
Reading
1. B; 2. C; 3. A; 4. D; 5. C

Strategy: Understanding Connotation
6. C; 7. B; 8. A; 9. C; 10. B

Vocabulary
11. agoraphobia; 12. irrational; 13. free association;
14. distinguish; 15. anonymous; 16. outburst;
17. amnesia; 18. motive; 19. dizziness; 20. severe

Mechanics
21. was brought; 22. having; 23. In addition;
24. expressed; 25. Moreover; 26. was hospitalized;
27. However; 28. be released; 29. wants;
30. Moreover

Editing

Cognitive behavioral therapy is a form of psychological therapy that ~~bases~~ ^is based^ ∧ on the ways in ~~that~~ ^which^ ∧ our thinking affects how we feel and what we do. Therapists ~~which~~ ^who^ ∧ use this approach help their patients replace the ways of thinking that are causing problems. One benefit to this approach is that we can change our thoughts much more easily than we can change a situation. In CBT, people are

encouraged to remain calm in bad situations.
We will always have bad situations; however ∧
when we become upset about the situation,
we have two problems rather than one.
Remaining calm ~~is avoided~~ *avoids* ∧ one of those
problems.

Chapter 7
Reading
1. B; 2. C; 3. A; 4. C; 5. D

Strategy: Finding Sentences with Similar Meanings
6. B; 7. C; 8. C; 9. B; 10. B

Vocabulary
11. abstinence; 12. epidemic; 13. negligible;
14. craved; 15. confidential; 16. culinary; 17. rely on;
18. transmission; 19. relapse; 20. inhalant

Mechanics
21. If I didn't have a new job, I wouldn't make more money.
22. If he didn't smoke a lot, he wouldn't often get sick.
23. If we had reservations, we could eat there.
24. If I didn't belong to Alcoholics Anonymous, I wouldn't be sober.
25. If heroin weren't injected, the health risks wouldn't be (as/so) great.
26. If tobacco were controlled effectively, cigarette use wouldn't be increasing in developing countries.
27. If I studied enough, I would make good grades.
28. If the weather weren't so beautiful, we wouldn't be at the beach today.
29. If health care weren't good, people wouldn't live longer now.
30. If you didn't smoke, you wouldn't be 15 times more likely to get lung cancer.

Editing
  In the U.S., the tobacco industry is a
wealthy and powerful group. However, it is

time the government did more to regulate
tobacco or make it illegal, ~~since~~ *although/even though* ∧ many
people would protest such controls on their
cigarettes. If tobacco ~~was~~ *were* ∧ illegal, it ~~will~~ *would* ∧
be much harder for young people to begin
smoking. Also, more smokers ~~will~~ *would* ∧ be
motivated to quit. Unless we take strong
action ∧ ᴾP̸eople will continue to become
addicted.

Chapter 8
Reading
1. A; 2. C; 3. D; 4. B; 5. D

Strategy: Hedging
6. A; 7. B; 8. B; 9. A; 10. B

Vocabulary
11. hypertension; 12. obesity; 13. placebo;
14. chronic; 15. wear down; 16. hostility;
17. baffling; 18. quack; 19. device; 20. integrate

Mechanics
21. may; 22. but; 23. As a result; 24. Although;
25. might not; 26. However; 27. so; 28. Even so;
29. can; 30. must

Editing
  Dr. Herbert Benson has written a number of
books, including /*The Relaxation Response*/ "The Relaxation Response. ∧
Dr. Benson, in studies at Harvard, found that
just as activity in one part of the brain can
activate the " fight or flight response / ∧ " ∧
activating other parts of the brain can
reduce/ stress and relax the body. He
suggests that repeating a word or an activity,
~~for~~ *and* ∧ consciously ignoring distracting

thoughts and stimuli, will activate these other parts of the brain. ~~Even so~~ As a result, this process causes a "relaxation response."

 **CREDITS**

Text Credits

p. T5: "The U.S. Economy" adapted from Roger LeRoy Miller, *Economics: Today and Tomorrow.* Copyright © 1995, 1991 by Glencoe/McGraw-Hill. Reprinted with the permission of the McGraw-Hill Companies. p. T13: "High-Tech Pyramid" adapted from Gene A. Mittler, *Art in Focus.* Copyright © 1994 by Glencoe/McGraw-Hill. Reprinted with the permission of the McGraw-Hill Companies. p. T21: "What Causes Schizophrenia?" adapted from Richard A. Kasschau, *Understanding Psychology.* Copyright © 1995 by Glencoe Publishing Company. Reprinted with the permission of the McGraw-Hill Companies. p. T25: "Codependency" adapted from Mary Bronson Merki and Don Merki, *Health: A Guide to Wellness.* Copyright © 1994 by Glencoe/McGraw-Hill. Reprinted with the permission of the McGraw-Hill Companies.